WALKING
WITH
GHOSTS

WALKING WITH GHOSTS

A MEMOIR

Gabriel Byrne

Grove Press
New York

FIRST EDITION

Printed in Canada

First Grove Atlantic edition: January 2021

Text Design by Norman E. Tuttle at Alpha Design & Composition
This book was set in 11.75-pt. Stempel Garamond by
Alpha Design & Composition of Pittsfield, NH.

ISBN 978-0-8021-5712-6
eISBN 978-0-8021-5714-0

Grove Press
an imprint of Grove Atlantic
154 West 14th Street
New York, NY 10011

Distributed by Publishers Group West

groveatlantic.com

21 22 23 24   10 9 8 7 6 5 4 3 2 1

For Hannah, my love

Fear not for the future, weep not for the past.
—Percy Bysshe Shelley (1792–1822)

WALKING WITH GHOSTS

HOW MANY TIMES have I returned in my dreams to this hill. It is always summer as I look out over the gold and green fields, ditches foaming with hawthorn and lilac, river glinting under the sun like a blade. When I was young, I found sanctuary here and the memory of it deep in my soul ever after has brought me comfort. Once I believed it would never change, but that was before I came to know that all things must. It's a car park now, a sightseers panorama.

Here, I imagined my life to come, read my comics, later forbidden paperbacks. Once, a book of one thousand jokes, which I tried to learn by heart so people would like me for making them laugh. Two cannibals are eating a clown. One says to the other: Does this taste funny to you?

I dreamed of first love. A dark-haired girl with pale skin. How I loved Mary Foley in her pink cardigan, smiling. For her I would ride my invisible horse to the doors of Wild West saloons, shoot at Nazi stormtroopers, and score the winning goal for Ireland in the final moment of extra time. Alas, she loved another. Elvis Presley.

I would come here in all seasons, when grass was stiff with frost or on days of such stillness you could hear the fwoofing wings of a pheasant startled from a bush.

Autumn, and the earth turned, evenings drew in, fires were lit in front rooms. The smell of earth in decay, smoke from burning leaves carried on the wind, and a kind of melancholy that made me lonely.

On winter evenings electric wires sang like ghosts in the laneways. The beams of an occasional car lit the bare-fingered trees as I ran to the farm to collect milk for my mother, who distrusted shop-bought.

The old farmer woman sat on a one-legged stool, milk foaming into the bucket between her legs, her head leaning against their ribs, cow piss running out into the yard, their flanks caked with dried shit like scabs, letting out bellows as they looked at you, sad-eyed.

Sometimes for a joke she would turn their teats and spray us as we ran for cover. Jews came too for their milk, carrying silver cans, speaking their own strange language.

Then, like a forgotten memory stirring, springtime arrived again, dark giving way to light. Windows opened, the first snow-drops and daffodils and coltsfoot appeared; evenings lengthened; all of nature stretching after its long sleep. Days that brought joy and hope.

Finally, the longed-for summer: the sky blue as the Virgin Mary's mantle, long days of freedom from hated school.

I am thinking of the seasons of my own life, learning now in my winter days I must shed what I have held most dear.

Yet there is contentment, even joy, in a landscape of bare trees, when the light makes everything more stark and bittersweet.

Here I stand now, a man longing to see as a child again, when every smell and sound and sight was a marvel. Yet I will never know again the childhood thrill of finding a hawk feather snagged on a briar, or the taste of wild blackberries after rain.

This place birthed my love of simple things.

I have never loved concrete as I love a tree, or reeds by a river flamed by an evening sun, or the first stars of evening; the bleat of a lamb in a distant field or the small spitter of rain on a windowpane.

Sometimes in those days I felt that I might crack and break apart with joy, and to contain my wild feelings I ran and summersaulted until I was breathless and dizzy. I lay for hours beneath the upside-down sea of the sky, where the clouds became camels or the face of God.

Over there a boat rotted by the riverbank where long-beaked birds speared for food. I liked to stand and sing on the river stones, bare feet distorted by cold rushing water. When rain came, I'd take shelter in the hoof-marked mud beneath the trees. I shat there like the animals, wiped myself with a dock leaf, covered it in case anyone might know it was mine.

Here is the ruin of a small cottage where Mrs. Doran lived alone. Her husband had been a soldier. One day he left in his green uniform on his motorbike and never came back again. There was still a photograph of him on the mantelpiece beside the one-eyed china cat.

That's where Mrs. Prunty used to live in her great house. Only the chimneys showed above the woods where her family had resided since before the famine. We hardly ever saw her, except in the fields tending to her horses, moving among them with a bucket of feed, touching their faces as they whinnied and stomped and butted heads in delight. Or on Sundays in the back of the old Bentley, face covered by a mantilla, being driven to service in the Protestant church.

Once, we stole through the woods and peered in through the lace curtains at the furniture covered with sheets, buckets on the floor to catch the rain from a leaking roof, the Bechstein piano we had seen speeding above the hedgerows on Turley's truck, rotting in a corner.

Beyond is the chapel, its door locked now with a thick chain. When I was a child, it was always open, God's house, for a quick prayer. Another place of escape and comfort, where I came for the answers to what ailed my boyhood self. A little chat with Himself. The recording of a bell rings now from its tower. Beyond was the factory where once the workers poured in and out of the gates to the siren's call. Men in boilersuits, women in nylon smocks and headscarves.

It's a block of expensive-looking apartments now.

Across the field was the dance hall, by day an unremarkable building of cement with peeling paint doors.

But by night, lit by Christmas lights around the door, it was a place of magic. From a ways off you'd hear the music spilling out over the fields.

Crowds streaming out of the pubs, some walking or on bicycles; hard chaws in their fathers' cars leaning out windows with cigarettes, like they were in a film, combing oiled hair into Elvis quiffs and whistling at the girls click-clacking by in short dresses.

On the stage the spangle-suited band, brass flashing, guitars twanging beneath revolving globes that scattered shards of light over the dancers.

Wallflowers looked out with shy, uncertain eyes.

How long had they spent in front of the mirror getting ready and here they sat unwanted, with thumping hearts, yet hopeful they might be chosen, having to look unconcerned when they were not.

I understood them, afraid of being rejected, as I was shoved toward them in a herd of Brut aftershave and Guinness.

There was a row of shops, I remember.

On the corner, the hardware shop where grumpy Tom, in canvas coat, sold everything from rat poison to Christmas candles, nothing a bother.

And the drapery where Betty worked. My mother bought her Castle Hosiery nylons and satin underthings there.

I liked to watch Betty in her nylon coat, beehive hair tied with a ribbon, pins in her mouth; moving around the shop in high heels. I could see the outline of her underwear and the little notches of her stockings. My first sins of impurity.

Next door was Mr. O. the chemist and part-time waltzer.

Open nine sharp, closed five on the dot. Fresh starched white jacket every day, three buttons on the shoulder, name written in red across the chest.

He'd give my mother medicine in a little white envelope, to help her sleep when she'd go up for her lie-down in the afternoons with the curtains closed.

—Maureen O'Hara herself couldn't hold a candle to your mother, he'd say.

At the end of the row there was Bill the barber's.

Bill had worn a wig for fifty years. A formal one for Sunday Mass. An untidier one for more casual occasions. If you happened to call to his house, he might have on his after-bath piece.

—Come in, I'm just drying me hair!

A ladies' man, quick with a wink or saucy word, he'd saunter down the street in his David Niven mustache and Crombie overcoat.

I loved his cozy shop of red-vinyl-and-chrome chairs, colored bottles and shaving mugs with the Queen's face, sticky paper with dead flies hanging from the ceiling, a fog of cigarette smoke. Ash from his cigarette falling into the gap between your neck and shirt, the cold clippers catching, pushing your head down, him blowing at you with his hot breath and your hair falling to the floor in clumps, and Gerry, his apprentice, sweeping it into a bag to be brought to a place where they made wigs for sick people.

Maybe that's where Bill got his made; he could have been wearing my hair.

And the victualler's.

MEAT TO PLEASE YOU, PLEASED TO MEET YOU, a sign said under a drawing of a pig dressed like a man with trousers and a jacket.

Where the butcher chopped up bad boys, made them into dog food; gristle, bone, organs, and all.

Then the picture house, Hollywood dreams on a white screen. The creaking of seats as lovers kissed and fumbled under coats. I saw sometimes ten films a week in a fog of cigarette smoke and disinfectant. There I am in its womb, dark refuge.

At the crossroads every Monday, the men pasted the coming attractions for the week on the hoarding, the smell of geraniums rising up from the hedges around it.

My grandmother brought me the first time to the pictures.

Photographs of film actors smiled at me as I ascended the stair in the echoing dark like a blind boy, holding onto her coat.

A curtain of snow trees covered the screen and there were soft glassed lights above in a ceiling of stars, and the red-uniformed ushers walked up and down the aisles. A girl in a yellow coat sold ice cream and chocolate from a tray.

Then it was dark and a huge ocean tumbled toward us, horses thundered through dust and gunshots, a woman screamed and a man was dying in her arms and sad music played.

But always the wonder and magic leaked away and the world dulled, as if drained of color and sound, when we came out into the ordinary street again.

But how I loved this world of imagination my grandmother opened for me.

Cold-eyed killers moved in the shadows, singing cowboys pushed through saloon doors, stubbled American soldiers dangled cigars from the sides of their mouths, and screaming Indians riding bareback were shot down to die spectacularly in the dust by the cavalry heroes in blue. There were women with pointed breasts, the circus, funny men, swords and spaceships, Arabia, Paris, St. Louis, the North Pole.

Once, the excitement of seeing Dublin on the screen, and we gave it a round of applause for being Dublin.

And grandmother used to marvel at how in old films all the people you saw on the screen were dead and were ghosts now. And she would pick out a random person in the background and say what a strange thing to be captured by a film crossing the street years later among a crowd of anonymous people.

The picture house is a carpet showroom now.

I stood yesterday where the screen would have been.

—If I can be of any assistance, sir? Was there anything in particular you were looking for? the salesman asked.

—There used to be an usher dressed in red braided uniform to click your ticket. Right where you're standing. And the stairways had photographs of the stars.

Glamorous and godlike. Beyond imagining.

And look up there: where the houses of the new estates are now, the road to the countryside once began. Farms on either side, orchards, fields of barley and corn.

I remember my father teaching me to ride a bicycle in the laneways among the high hedges. I wobbled and tumbled into the ditch, and he made me get up again, and soon I was speeding down the hill, the wind in my face, and one day I reached the bottom without falling and I let out a whoop of joy and soon I was riding down with my feet on the handlebars. And I wished everyone would see me, especially Mary Foley, and be full of admiration for me being so brave and heedless of danger.

My father taught me how to read simple things: the bundling of clouds, or the seconds between thunder and lightning to tell how far it is away. How to smell snow in the wind and know by the night sky if frost will come.

He taught me the names of trees, wildflowers, birds.

I remember a day, standing beneath the trees to take shelter from the rain, my father and I watched a field being plowed. The horses plodding through the black turned earth, backs slick with rain, a man walking behind them.

Hike, he said when he wanted them to stop and *Gup,* when he wanted them to go on.

Crows and gulls circled and shrieked, grub-greedy on the air behind. Beyond the field, a rain curtain covered the mountain. The man turned the beasts at the end of the field, the blade catching the light and flashing.

A sudden wind came up, making leaves flap like the wings of insects, and just as suddenly the sun came out and then the last drops like when you pop your lips together and the hills were clear again. A rainbow appeared in the blue-black sky.

The horses put their heads together and made a noise like a sneeze. The man held the shaft of the plow, straining this way and that, cutting into the black earth. Once, they made a mistake and he pulled them back; they stomped their heavy hooves and started again. One had a white stripe on his face, as if painted there, the other had white socks. The long strips of cut earth narrowed the field with each turn, and the man stopped to light a cigarette out of the wind's way as the animals munched from nosebags, having their dinner and a rest.

—He is the last of his kind, my father said.

I carry that day like a photograph in my heart.

I had never felt so close to him as in that silence.

Here I come to a bridge that crosses a four-lane motorway now cutting through those fields, see the blue lights of a police car, kids being handcuffed by the embankment.

—Too bloody soft on them, a man with a dog says. A few lashes of the cat-o'-nine tails. That would put manners on them.

I move along, to the house that was our home, where eight of us lived for so many years. How the hell did we all fit in there?

Gone my father's hedge that he clipped on summer evenings. The grass he cut, pushing the mower over and back, whistling to himself. The flowers that bordered the path replaced by concrete. The curtains my mother bought because Mrs. Kelly, the doctor's wife, had the same ones.

I can see her standing in the living room to appraise them.

Mrs. Kelly was the first to get a Hoover and you'd see her out in flowered housecoat and fluffy slippers, on the porch sucking at the dirt with the nozzle and changing the brushes for the mats. Her door would be open and opera pouring out from the record player and you could see into the hallway, and her white table with the telephone there, a painting of a crying boy above.

—Lino isn't good enough for that one.

I can see my father too, in his years of unemployment sitting behind those curtains, smoking his pipe, watching the theater of the street.

Friday nights: my sisters made-up and glamorous, hurrying to meet boyfriends. Commandeering bathrooms, clothes drying before the fire. Us boys, hair oiled, covered in Brut aftershave, the record player or the radio at full blast.

—I'll take a hammer to that curse of God music, my father used to say.

The front door opens now, and a man and woman step out, pushing a pram. I look behind them for a moment into an open-plan extension where our kitchen used to be. The man regards me with suspicion.

—You want something?

—No, nothing. Just looking. I used to live here.

They pull the gate behind them and walk down the street without a backward glance. And I stand, an intruder in my own past. I think of our life there, all the days and all the nights since. The weeks, the months, the years. I think of time, and how it passes.

IT WAS WINTER, New York. I was an exile emigrant and immigrant, belonging everywhere and nowhere at all. Home is where the heart is but the heart itself had no home. Last leaves clung to trees, the roofs of the townhouses were wet with rain, the lights of the traffic a blur of red blossoms. Buildings like huge gravestones rising into the night. In the distance the ghosts of the trade towers haunted the city.

I had rented an apartment in a skyscraper. I could see into the surrounding apartments. Sometimes I felt as if I was watching films with the sound turned off.

I have always found refuge in imagination. As a child I would escape hurt and loneliness by taking refuge in stories I would create for myself. Later as an adult when I found my identity shattered by sorrow or even success, when I didn't know who I was, I retreated into a world of imagining.

On this evening, there were fireworks, and the world danced. The sky exploded with lights, left glittering trails behind. Twenty-three floors down stood a clothing store on the corner, and in the window's arctic landscape, a mannequin bride stood forlorn, eyes downcast toward her artificial flowers. Her lover had fled, leaving her all alone in this alien place. Behind her, a flock of merry penguins in top hats and tails twirled canes. I imagined the sad-faced bride and her penguins dancing out of the window, down the avenue.

A balloon headed skyward as if fleeing the world below. A father spun his baby in a dance, as the mother waited a few steps further on, pram full of groceries. In the apartment building opposite mine, a boy practiced piano, flicking the pages of music in a room of pink walls and abstract sculpture. Alerted to the sounds of fireworks, he came to the balcony and was lost in wonder as the sky filled with palm trees and golden snakes, fairy dust and witches' hair, sea creatures the color of emeralds. All falling into nothingness.

People in the street moved on, having been children again for a few moments. Opposite, an apartment was being painted by men in white overalls. I imagined them dancing in slow motion among the covered furniture to unheard music. On a balcony, a girl sat, legs atop a table, and shared a joint with her boyfriend, her face obscured by windswept hair. The next apartment, the man who never slept. At all hours of the night I would see him lean on his balcony smoking, casual as a farmer leaning over a gate. And way, way below, a man tried to capture the wind in a plastic bag.

I was about to draw the blinds.

A door in an apartment below opened. A man and a woman fell through, kissing, tearing at each other's clothes. I hesitated, turned off the light and watched them tumble to the bed. Afterward, she walked in a sheet to the bathroom. He lay on the bed, remote control in his hand. He found a news channel. She moved from the bathroom to the kitchen, opening cupboards, taking out coffee. He lit a cigarette. She brought him a cup, took a drag of his smoke. Leaned over to kiss him. She came to the window and looked out for a moment.

Did she see me standing in the dark of my living room?

She seemed to look straight at me, then she pulled the curtain closed.

Later, I was seated at the bar of a restaurant on my block. The couple came in and sat across from me. The girl looked at me and whispered something to her boyfriend. He emptied a handful of peanuts into his mouth.

—Hey, dude we know you, right? You live in the neighborhood? No, that's not it, it's from somewhere else. You look very familiar.

—I got it, she said, excited. He was in a movie, right? What was the name of it? This is going to drive me crazy. It is him, isn't it? I know I've seen him before.

And I've seen you before, I thought.

—He's so familiar, isn't he? she said to her man.

—C'mon dude, tell us. Who are you?

◦❀◦

I was born shortly after my parents met. They first saw one another on a night in November in 1948. My father recalled:

—I ran away from home to the city as quick as ever I could. I wanted more than just laboring for the big farmers, snagging turnips out in all weather. So I joined the army to see the world. Never got beyond Dublin, that's how far I got. Till that night I took shelter in the doorway and your mother was standing beside me and I wanted to talk to her, but I was a bit timid and didn't want to be too forward and I couldn't think of anything to say. Then I saw her with no matches for her cigarette and that was my in. I knew she was for me. We got married in Westland Row church shortly after, and in less than a year, into the world we brought you.

My mother told me:

—We used to play tennis and go to dances on our nights off, at the Metropole mostly. All the nurses did. It had a grand ballroom and a good orchestra and was always stuffed to the gills. One night I was coming in on the bus to meet a few of the girls for something to eat in Wynn's Hotel before the dance. It wasn't done for women to be seen smoking on the bus so I hopped off a stop before the bridge. It started to rain and the next thing, I was in the doorway of a shop and rooting in my handbag for matches and this fellow in an army uniform leaned over with a match and his hand over the flame. We got talking and it turned out he was off to the Metropole as well. We danced that night and we met the next week and that was it for good and all. It was our fate to meet like that because of the rain and the matches and the Metropole and the doorway, and if it hadn't happened like that you might not be here now. Isn't that a strange thing to think? The way we all come into the world.

❧⸿❧

—You gave the fight not to come, but out you landed in the end. And you didn't like it one bit. The red puss on you, and the baldy head, not a lick of hair; upside down and a slap on the arse to set you roaring. O the bawls of you! The whole country kept wide awake. Three o'clock in the morning in the Rotunda Hospital there beside the Gate Theatre. Lying later on my shoulder, eyes shut tight, sleeping like a kitten. O, but a cranky lump if you didn't get a sup of the breast.

Wrapped in the christening shawl that was my own grandmother's—do you remember that shawl? The loveliest thing. Made by a blind nun in Scotland. My own mother was christened in it and it did duty for all six of you. Three boys, three girls. The same priest pouring the water over your heads. You the first. When I'd start to show, the neighbors would be saying, Time to get the shawl ready, Mrs. B. Six was a small family for that time. Mrs. Brown beyond had twenty-three children. The poor creature. She used to say the only holiday she ever got was the ten days above in the maternity hospital. Then back to slaving and trying to keep body and soul together and a roof over their heads.

We ferried you home in your uncle's vegetable van, driving like a snail so as not to disturb your majesty, till home safe and sound all the neighbors come in for a good gawk with their rawmaish and pass, remarking:

The spit of his mother!

A pure dote is what he is!

And yourself there gummy and scrunched up like an old man's fist. But Lord, you were so beautiful to me.

Always mad about the women, the soft pillows of their chests; bouncing you on their knees in your plastic knickers, teetertottering from one to the other, inhaling their sweet perfume. The widdy woman from next door singing her own favorite songs, as she would often. Didn't like the smell of cigarettes and whiskey off the men or stubbly faces rough against your own; hairy tattooed arm inked in blue one of them had, and you'd run away from him like a scalded cat.

Next-door Peggy wheeling you in the pram along the street. She'd be showing you off like little Lord Fauntleroy; strangers gandering in at you in your pointy pink hat. You were so amazed and delighted with the world, waddling drunkenly after the birds, touching the wet nose of a dog, tasting ice cream for the first time from Peggy's scarlet fingernail.

I remember you in the garden along the path between the vegetables. Your father digging in the black clay, and myself hanging clothes on the line, a basket at my hip and pegs in my mouth. Spying you with my little eye. Nothing would do you but eating the clay, and I had to give you a little slap. Spit that out! Bold boy. You crying, afraid, because you didn't know that eating clay is a bold thing. Your father leaning on his spade laughing, and me carrying you upside down into the kitchen. And I locked you into the baby chair and washed your mouth and I couldn't help smiling because you were such a good boy. Except when you did bold things.

Flowers at the edge of the grass.

—You tried to eat their colors and smells.

Clip clip, snip snip, leaves fell as my father cut the hedge. People passed on the pathway and spoke to him, smiled at him.

I crawled to a ball, red on the green grass, and it moved, and I pushed it again.

I chased the sun across the garden, trying to hold its beams in my fingers. The breeze was like a small breath on my face. Voices and music streamed out of the windows of the neighbors' houses. Children played and skipped in the street beyond. They sang:

In and out go darkly bluebells
In and out go darkly bluebells
In and out go darkly bluebells
So early in the morning.

Mother said:

—You listened to them sing, but you didn't understand, so you'd say "dadlubel" over and over to make your own little rhyme of it.

Grass grew cold, shadows lengthened.

I remember flames leaping, lovely and yellow, up the chimney. My father played my favorite game, horsey-horsey. Bounced me up and down on his leg. First slow, then faster and faster until his horsey knees were galloping. And I held on tight to the reins of his belt, then tumbled down between his legs. I wanted to do horsey again and again. Over and over and over and over.

—A pure devil for the horsey-horsey, my father would say.

On either side of the fire sat Mother and Father, speaking to each other. Then it was up the wooden hill to "Bedford," which is what they called the stairs and bed.

—I'd sing you a song, a lullaby, she said.

Hear the wind blow love
O hear the wind blow
Currachs are sailing
Way out on the blue.

Holy God, putting out the lights in the world and listening to the voices of all the people. Mine, too. There in stripy jim-jams, I'd kneel on the cold linoleum as my own guardian angel stood by the bed. Even if I couldn't see him I knew he was there, wings folded to protect me from all the dangers of the night.

—Good night trees good night stars good night moon good night clouds.

Then: the scaredy-cat dark. The radio on downstairs, low sounds of voices by the fire, eyes heavy now. A dog barking in a shed next door. The long day ending as I tumbled down into sleep.

Another morning beginning.

Light and dark. Dark and light. So the days and the nights passed, and I was happy in small things as I came to know the world.

Then, out of nowhere, changes happened.

—It was almost Christmas when we moved to our new house, said Mother. Nighttime.

I remember rain slanting under the streetlights as we crossed the bridge over the river, passing strange houses, televisions turning rooms blue. Christmas trees and paper stars in hallways. Mother pushed the pram loaded with kettles and pots, rain soaking her headscarf with horses on it. Father was working late. A bus passed full of people dry and warm, rubbing the windows to look out.

—Why do we have to leave our house?

—Because. That's the why, Father said.

—Because it's for the best, Mother said.

—You'll like where we are moving. There's fields and cows and horses and shops and everything, and you can see the mountains from the back window.

—I don't want to go.

Mother remembered that I lay down on the floor and roared and hammered the floorboards with my fists.

—The temper on you would frighten the daylight out of a person.

She pulled back the bolt of the gate and I saw the new house for the first time. It had no smile for me. She found a key under the mat and then we were in a dark hallway, loud with new silence and a smell of cold. She found a light. The walls had holes, newspaper covered the floors. I did not like this place, and I began to cry again for my old home, and my bedroom over the garden and monkey tree, the doors and the windows and the pathway and the scrapy gate and the old widdy woman and next-door Peggy.

The moon slid over the walls and down the stairs. I lay on a mattress on the floor, bundled in overcoats to keep warm. Through the window, I could make out the shape of a hill like a crouched animal, waiting to get me.

And then, my life changed again. My new brother arrived, wrapped in my hand-me-down christening shawl.

My mother said:

—And of course, what did your majesty here do? Only lie down on the floor and roar the head off yourself.

I can still see the fear in my father's face. He ran from the room, calling for my mother.

—O Lord, o Lord, God-blessed Jesus and His holy mother, save us.

They were both looking at me with afraid faces. Then anger faces. My brother watched me too, dribble coming from his mouth. They forced a spoon into it. Then the quilt was covered in vomit.

Father held up a small bottle of turpentine.

—He tried to poison the baby.

He turned to face me. I was scared then. My mother was rocking my roaring brother in her arms, and a strange man with a black bag looked at me. He was Dr. Kelly.

—I was painting the wall, my father said, and I left the bottle of turpentine down. I turn around and I see him upending it into the baby's mouth. What are we to do with him at all, Doctor? Father said.

—What are we to do with him at all? Mother repeated.

The man with his black bag left.

—Tell your brother you're sorry for trying to kill him.

My brother gurgled and laughed, showing his one tooth. He didn't mind that I tried to murder him.

Every morning in childhood, the radio would wake me, its crackly BBC voices from London carried over the Irish Sea and into the kitchen. My father would talk back to it as he shaved.

—Well God bless your honor and your honor's horse, he'd say.

Up the bare stairs he'd come, bringing tea to Mother.

—Let the dog see the rabbit.

A creaking of springs and laughter.

On this morning, Father entered my room, made the sign of the cross on my forehead to keep me safe for the day. It was September 1955, and my first day of school.

I was dressed in a navy suit and new leather boots with steel tips and a badge with a heart on my coat. I was sick with fear. My father had taught me to count with apples and to draw numbers.

—One is a line, two is a swan, three is a pig's tail.

Now I had to go to school to learn other things. The night before, Mother made me take a bath and said that every child had to go to school.

—Why?

—That's the why. You have to learn to read and write and add up sums so you can make your way in the world. You don't want to grow up to be a dunderhead and not know *b* from a bull's foot. Once you get a few days of it under your belt, you won't want to come home at all, she said.

I'll buy me child a saucepan
I'll buy me child a spoon
I'll buy me child a writing set
So he can go to school.

I held tight to Mother's dress while she baked tomorrow's bread, the sweet smell filling the house, her hands covered in flour. She made a little dough man specially for me from the leftover flour. She lit up a cigarette, and all the tension went out of her, the smoke rising like a blue ghost. I liked when she smoked because she always fell into a good humor and would tell me a story.

—Will I tell you a story about Johnny Magory? she asked. Will I begin it? Well that's all that's in it, she said, laughing. It was a joke story to cheer me up, because she knew I was worried about school.

In the dark morning, we waited for the bus. People stomped their feet to keep warm in the wind and rain. A broken umbrella blew along the road like a huge spider. I remembered a picture in a book once, a baby in the sky with fat cheeks who puffed at tree leaves. That was the wind baby who lived beyond the clouds. But I was big now, so I didn't believe in the wind baby.

At last, the bus arrived. Mother and I squeezed and pushed onto the platform. The conductor with the high voice—the one everybody called Mary even though he was a man—told us:

—Come on now, push up the car there, please, ladies and germs.

And we found ourselves on the long television seat which faced everyone. I looked out at my familiar streets falling away, rain running down the windows.

My face burned because people were looking at me in my new uniform that itched my skin. I did not like to be looked at. Once, mother had to pull me out by the leg from under the bed when a neighbor called. I knew places to hide when I wanted to be alone: in the wardrobe, among Mother's skirts and coats, breathing in camphor and the scent of her perfume, or under the stairs where the gas meter was and where mice found homes in the pockets of old coats.

My face flamed red with shame when the woman beside me, who smelled of coal smoke and perfume, smiled at me. People looking at me always made me blush. A girl once said to me, Hey, give us a light off your face for me cigarette, and everyone laughed. I pretended to laugh too.

Once, going into town to the shops with Mother, there was a man in a coat too small for him who had no socks on and shoes with no laces. He was sitting on the television seat singing a song in Irish and the whole bus clapped when he finished.

—I think you're on the wrong bus, Brendan, said the conductor.

—Are youse not going to Crumlin? the man replied.

—Ah, no, this is the Drimnagh bus, Brendan. You should be on the number fifty.

He said goodbye to everyone as he came down the aisle.

—What age is the chiseler? he said to my mother, looking at me.

—He's almost five.

—Long life to him, missus.

—Watch your step now, Brendan.

The driver pushed back the glass door, waiting for him to get off. The man stood on the footpath saluting like a soldier.

—God bless Brendan. People turned to get a last look at him.

—That man, my mother said, is a famous writer. And he on the wrong bus, God love him, the creature.

We came to a redbrick building and entered a long hallway. I could hear the echo of our footsteps following us; a piano, and a voice, singing. There was a window: blue and red and green, with a girl saint who looked straight at me, and Patrick Pearse the Rebel, who was executed by the British in 1916, his gammy eye turned away so you couldn't see it.

A smell like rotten eggs came over the walls of the school on the wind. It was from O'Keefe's yard, where they killed animals to make shoes and rosary beads. They hosed the blood off the walls. You could hear the cows and horses roaring with fear for miles.

Once, in the country at my uncle's, I saw men pull a cow from a trailer by ropes. There was terror in her eyes and her hooves slipped, the men not caring. They hit her hard across her back and legs with sticks till they had her in the shed and she was screaming and crying in her cow way. One of them put a kind of gun to her forehead and she fell down in a twitching heap and they pulled her out along the ground, thoughtless as to whether she banged her head, laughing and joking as if her pain were nothing at all.

Sometimes, Father would bring home herring in blood-stained newspaper for dinner on the carrier of his bike. The dead eyes of the fish made me wonder if they felt pain. What a thing to be caught by a hook on the inside of your mouth, to die gasping for air, then to be eaten by a human. He fried them in flour and butter in the pan, cut off the tails and the heads, which he threw out the back door to the cat.

Often, there were rabbits and turkeys and chickens, life drained from them, hanging from a nail on our kitchen door. I stared at them, wondering if they knew they had died or whether they ever missed being alive. Sometimes, for a laugh, Mother would chase us around the house in a bedsheet waving a yellow withered claw as we laughed and screamed up the stairs and through the rooms, until she trapped us and we felt the dead claw on our skin.

I held tighter to Mother's hand, her ring against my fingers. I was afraid I would wet myself when a nun appeared, white plastic wings out from her head, the rest of her in black. Some boys stood and stared as if they were scared, like me. Mother wet her fingers to comb my hair and pinned a Miraculous Medal to the inside of my coat.

—That's so Our Blessed Lady will look after you and keep you safe from all harm.

The nun's face was cross as she formed us into lines. One of the nuns held a boy by the ear.

—Get into that line you or you'll see what's good for you.

I hid behind Mother's coat as the nun reached us.

—What is this boy's name, tell me?

Mother told her.

—He has an Angel's name, said the nun.

Mother told me once how I got my name.

—It was when you were floating inside me, in your own little world. One afternoon, I was that tired I decided to have a bit of an early lie-down. The next thing, I woke up in a kind of sweat and something made me go to the window and I saw it was already nighttime. I was cooling my forehead against the glass and didn't it start to snow. Big thick flakes of it, falling on

the trees and the grass. The whole garden white and bits of dia-
monds shining here and there under the light of the moon and
the shadows of branches. And what did I see but a shape coming
out of the snow with wings, moving silently up and down, and
didn't it land beyond on the bicycle shed. Well, the heart went
crossways in me. It started tapping with a wing on the window.

Are you a ghost or what are you at all? says I.

Oh, and he gave me a smile, it was the loveliest, kindest
smile I ever saw. What was he? Only an angel.

And even though he didn't speak a word, I understood that
he was telling me the name I should call you. Then he disappeared back into the snow, not a trace of him when I woke again
and I looked out into the garden, true as I'm standing here, there
wasn't a trace of snow either.

So I knew that it was a fever dream I was after having. And
I said your name for the first time, to myself, out loud.

The sister took me away with the waxy flesh of her hand, and
when I looked back, there was only emptiness where Mother
had been. She was gone.

—Do you remember? Mother said. You showed me the
moon you drew that very first day, a white balloon. A man's
face in it. And a house, smoke coming from the chimney, a hill
behind it and a dog in front and a monkey puzzle tree. The dog
was bigger than the house and that made us laugh. And there
was a river running before it. And a rain barrel to the side, a pipe
coming from the roof and a tree bending over it, and a pathway
with a gate to the door. Even curtains on the windows. That's
my home, you said.

We were seated, silent, row by row in a long room. A fire flamed
in the corner.

On the wall, Jesus was nailed to a cross with no clothes on except for a nappy. Blood spilled from his head, hands, and feet, where nails were hammered in.

She taught us a hymn, and every morning after, we sang it, as sad-faced Jesus, who was crucified for our sins, listened.

Soul of my savior
Sanctify my breast
Body of Christ, be thou
My saving guest
Deep in thy wounds, Lord
Hide and shelter me
So, shall I never, never part from thee.

I wondered if I could climb into the wounds of Jesus for shelter, hide in there behind black-red blood.

We sing-sang at our tables. I didn't like sums because they had no stories like Jonah swallowed up by a whale and living in his stomach for three days and nights. Or the Fenian warriors who ran from one end of Ireland to the other and only stopped for a feed of blackberries in Mullingar. I could never see numbers in my mind.

The sister would scratch marks on the page with a pen in silence as she called out our names. Her veil brushed against my face as she passed between the rows. She carried a belt, and she would slap it on the desk to make us afraid, so we dared not move or breathe. She wore a gold ring on her finger because she was married to God.

Our blessed Lord knows everything about everyone in the whole world, even your most secret thoughts. He is divine, which means he doesn't have to go to the toilet or even eat. He doesn't have to go to school.

—Does any boy know what a soul is? the sister asked.

We all stared back at her, afraid to say anything.

—I do, I hesitantly said. There is a factory in Heaven where babies come from, I said. They are all on a shelf and there is a little door in their backs and God puts your soul in there, it looks like the sole on a shoe, it is spotless white except for a stain called original sin which all babies are born with, and when your soul is inside you and becomes invisible you are ready to come down to the earth to be a human being.

—That's a good answer, she said. What is original sin? she asked.

—Has it something to do with an orange? offered the Goose Gavin, who sat beside me.

—We are all born with the stain of original sin, she said, and it can never be rubbed out, no matter how much we try. Once upon a time there was a beautiful garden created by God called Eden, filled with animals and with every kind of fruit and flower. A Catholic man and a woman were put in charge, and they were our first parents. God made Adam, our father, first, out of some mud, and when he was asleep God took one of Adam's ribs out and He made a woman called Eve, so that Adam wouldn't be lonely all by himself. And they were as happy as anything and had everything they could ever want. The only thing God said was, Make sure you don't eat any of those apples off that tree over there, and they promised Him they wouldn't. But they couldn't stop looking at the tree and thinking about the apples.

Sure one bite won't do us any harm, Adam.

No, Eve, don't! You'll get us thrown out. You heard what God said.

But she couldn't help herself and she picked the apple and had a bite. It was so delicious, she made Adam take one too, and they sat on the grass, munching away.

Suddenly, God opened up the sky and He put His head out and He had an awful angry face on Him.

The one thing I asked you not to do! he roared.

Adam and Eve started to cry and wail, but God was sick and tired of them and he pointed his finger at the gate of the garden.

Get out and don't come back. I'm putting a curse on you to wander the world for all time. And by the way, your children will be miserable as well.

They looked down and realized they had no clothes on, and they were mortified with the shame and had to cover their private things with leaves.

That's why the world is such an unhappy place, the sister concluded, all because of Eve making Adam take a bite of an apple. So anytime you feel sad, it's because your soul knows it has been happy once, in the beautiful garden called Eden. We can never return because of the bad woman called Eve who tempted Adam.

—What is the Holy Ghost? she asked another day.

—Sometimes, Sister, one of the boys said, the Holy Ghost comes down on the earth disguised as a pigeon. Like the time when He was telling the Virgin Mary she was going to have a baby, because she didn't know. The pigeon has a kind face and sits on a windowsill with a halo around his head like in our catechism book.

She shouted at him:

—The Holy Ghost is a dove. Not a common dirty pigeon off the street.

The sister told us we were lucky because Ireland is a Catholic country.

—And that's because of St. Patrick, who is Ireland's patron saint. When St. Patrick came to our island to convert the Irish pagans, he told them there was no such thing as the gods of wind and gods of fire who lived under the earth; that the trees and rivers had no spirits living inside them. There was only one true God, but he had two other gods inside Him called the Holy Trinity, and to show them what he meant, he held up a shamrock with the three leaves on one stem. Immediately they had faith and didn't want to be pagans anymore. So, they converted to being Christians, which was what Catholics used to be called in the old days.

But the chieftains had one problem and they said maybe St. Patrick could help them solve it. The whole country of Ireland was infested with snakes. They were everywhere: in bushes, in the grass, in rivers, sneaking into people's bedrooms at night and biting them so that they died in agony. So St. Patrick took a big stick and he rooted out all the snakes from where they were hiding, heaps of them, twisting and spitting venom, and he banished them all into the sea where they drowned or swam over to England and other countries.

We sang a hymn to the statue of St. Patrick:

> *Hail glorious St. Patrick*
> *Dear saint of our isle*
> *On us thy poor children*
> *Bestow a sweet smile.*

But he never smiled, just stared at the snake crushed beneath his big knobbly foot.

THE FIRST TIME I came to Hollywood I checked into the Sunset Marquis Hotel, with its Hockneyesque garden of fragrant honeysuckle. Rabbits played in the grass and koi fish darted in the pools beneath jacaranda trees.

Richard Harris wandered barefoot in pee-stained linen trousers and an Irish rugby shirt. His wild hair blew out behind him like a mad creature of the forest.

—Is it too much to get a bowl of fucking porridge? he roared at a mahogany-tanned actor, who, reclining by the pool, repeated "porridge" as if it were a word from another language.

The Los Angeles heat had weakened my body. A blanket of smog hung low in the breezeless day. Melting in my room, I called the front desk:

—My room is lovely, but I'm roasting. Do you think you could send up a fan? The receptionist assured me she would attend to it immediately. An hour passed before the phone finally rang:

—I am sorry but I'm not having any luck. I've looked in the dining room and the garden and the pool area.

—I mean a fan for cooling the room . . . not, like, a human fan. There was a pause.

—I'm sorry, I'm new here.

I left my room and went down to the bar. I chatted with the waitress. Her name was Gloria, from Texas. She was dressed in a catsuit. I learned that she was studying to be an actress. She hated having to wear the catsuit.

—It's . . . whatever. My agent is getting me in rooms for projects now for pilot season. I like the job OK because they let me off to audition. You never know when your luck will change. One job is all it takes.

She had a reel: clips from a short she did, a commercial for a bank, some audition pieces.

—Sometimes I get depressed, she said. It's shitty being an out-of-work actor here. They promise you stuff, these guys, then you find out, you know, it's bullshit, they just want, you know. They think because we're dressed like this they can say anything to you. Hey baby nice legs! What time they open? Stuff like that.

The tanned actor called her over, his arms folded behind his head. He watched her as she moved toward him.

Night fell, and an odd melancholy engulfed me as I drove my rented car along Sunset Boulevard. Cars were backed up, thumping music from their interiors; neon advertisements along the boulevard for films coming out. Whiskey a Go Go.

In the Hollywood Hills, the roads were deserted. I imagined lonesome vampires, pale-faced in the moonlight, long, black cloaks lifted by the night wind. I drove up Benedict Canyon: road winding like a snake. My headlamps revealed cliffs of clay. I thought of Sharon Tate, seven months pregnant, murdered by the Manson gang. I parked the car and looked out over the pulsing lights of the San Fernando Valley.

I could not shake the sense of unease I had been feeling throughout the day. When I returned to the hotel, I went to the lounge for a drink. More catsuited girls with trays, but Gloria was not among them. I felt tired and returned to my room.

I stood on the balcony, breathing in the scent of orange and bougainvillea. A preacher like an Old Testament prophet was on television, reading the Bible—taking long pauses and puffing on a cigar, staring into the lens at sinners like me. A helicopter whirred above, its beam an angry cyclops among the gardens.

The people downstairs were having a party, the smell of marijuana drifted up with their laughter. Three girls were dancing in tight black dresses on the balcony, fingers clicking to the music, moving languidly to and from each other. It made me feel lonely, to be there by myself, watching them.

I fell asleep and had a dream that the world was ending. The old prophet from the television looked down from the sky, puffed on his cigar as the earth wobbled.

—You would not listen to me, he thundered, and I realized he was God. He flung me from him, a thing of no consequence.

My breath was coming fast in the dream, and the bed was shaking, as if being moved by giant hands in a rage, and I was thrown to the floor. The doors of the wardrobes rattled as if there were demons inside. The bedside lamp had toppled and set the room slantwise—the glass of the sliding doors shattered into a cobweb.

I attempted to stand but reeled, as if I were drunk, toward the doorway, where I crouched like a child warding off blows. I had never been so afraid. Glass was breaking. I thought, *I will die like this.*

The bedroom was in chaos. Glass strewn on the bed; the curtains blown inward; a chair impaled in the television screen; the minibar door ajar, bottles scattered about. That sound was the sloshing of the swimming pool. A scream.

The clock registered 4:29 a.m. The moon swam past in torn clouds on its way somewhere. People ran in the corridor. A British voice patrolled the hotel:

—Is everybody alright? The worst is over.

He reminded me of an air-raid warden in one of those old, black-and-white British films with that reassuring Cockney policeman voice.

I stood, but my legs went from underneath me.

The British man appeared in a red-checked dressing gown and fluffy, pink slippers. He helped me up and led me by the elbow into a foyer of flashlights and candles and people running forward and backward in the dark.

—Six-point-five, dude.

—No, it was a seven.

—It felt like a nine.

—Make way! yelled the air-raid warden, injured chaps here! There was comfort in giving ourselves over to his authority.

Everyone was in pajamas. I'd seen that woman this morning in the garden with her poodle cradled in her arms. And could that be Lulu? The singer? Or had my brain been injured?

Kenny G, weirdly, was still playing on the intercom.

The staff took charge. Order was being restored. A youth with blond curls was saying:

—My surfboard, dude! Got to get my surfboard!

Suddenly there was another violent shaking. We were passengers on the deck of a capsizing ship with gigantic waves beneath. I readied myself to die again.

Then, after an eternity of seconds, it ceased.

—Aftershock, the British leader proclaimed. There'll be a few of those. Nothing to frighten the French. The worst is over.

If this had been a movie, he would have been played by Kenneth More.

—Now, I suggest we all take the hand of the person either side of us, even if you can't see them.

I reached out and held the hand of the old woman with the dog. Lights came on and we all blinked, like children awoken from sleep, feeling slightly foolish, bonded by fear, and the joy of survival. The wolf hour was ending.

A voice boomed from the helicopter, ordering people to remain in their houses till the all clear was given. I remembered reading somewhere that in ancient Greece, rats, snakes, and weasels deserted the city of Helike before an earthquake destroyed it. Sensing the impending disaster, cats screeched and hens ceased to lay. This quake had only lasted twenty seconds. Fifty-seven people were killed, and nine thousand injured. The radio stations played "Concrete and Clay" by Unit 4 + 2, "Rock This Town" by Stray Cats, and "Whole Lotta Shakin' Goin' On" by Jerry Lee Lewis.

I was alive. I survived. Life had never seemed more precious. But I could never trust the ground beneath my feet again.

~ᘉᗪᗯᘉᗪᗯᘉᗪᗯ~

I remember when I first became aware of my own mortality. It was 1959. My father was working in the Guinness Brewery. The brewery smelled of things called yeast and hops which went into making black beer called porter. My father helped make wooden barrels. It took a lot of years to understand how to make a barrel and you had to have a special eye. When the barrels were full, they were loaded onto trucks. In the olden days, it would be a barge painted blue and yellow.

—I remember them well on the canal, the old boats puffing out big breaths of white smoke. And if you leaned on the bridge when they passed under, the smoke would make a ghost of you for a second. You'd hear the echo of the dogs barking under the bridge.

Arthur Guinness took care of his workers. Get a job in the brewery and bedad you're set for life. Sure where else would you get it? The free dentist and doctor and a swimming pool and a concert hall for the variety show every Christmas and your bonus and your pension? And don't forget the bicentennial while you're at it.

—What's a "boy centreeniel?" It was a hard word to say.

—It's a special day of celebrations. No work, no school, and everything is free. It's a present from the Guinness family to all their workers to celebrate another hundred years since it started.

—How long is a boy centreeniel?

—Twenty years multiplied by ten years, which equals two hundred.

Two hundred years. It was impossible to imagine, even if you drew a hundred lines on a page with a pencil.

—You better say a special prayer to St. Medard, Mother said.

—Who's he?

—The patron saint of the weather is who he is.

—Dear St. Medard, I prayed, you're probably very busy looking after the weather all over the world, but if it's not too much trouble, could you not let it rain in Dublin on the day of the boy centreeniel? Thank you.

Our good-day clothes were washed and ironed, shoes polished like mirrors before the fire, fingernails scrubbed, and we lay down sleepless, clean as whistles. And St. Medard answered our prayers. The lovely morning tapped on the window. There was a small breeze from under the broken window jamb.

My brother knocking on the bathroom door:

—Hurry up I'm bursting!

—Hold your horses, I just got in here.

The mad tumble down the stairs.

—Stop sliding on those bannisters, you'll get a chip in your arse.

—Did you wash your face, you dirtbird?

—Mister, you need to change your underpants before they walk out the door by themselves, said Mother.

—Are we ready, in the name of God?

—If we don't get a move on we'll be meeting ourselves coming back.

—Make sure the back door is locked.

—Are the lights off upstairs?

—Make sure there's no sparks in the grate or the house burned down on top of us.

—A nice howdoyoudo that would be, my father said.

The ordinary-day neighbors watching in envy. Mrs. Williams surgical stockinged, her new teeth like a row of fridges, leaning on her gate.

—Ye have the day for it, God bless it, she clicked. And Mr. Dowdall with his nobbly stick to frighten cats and teddy boys.

—Hooray, hooray, here comes the bus.

—Stand back, stand back, there's room for everyone.

—Here quit pushing.

—Are we all on?

—Take your head in.

—Heard of a lad once leaned out the window of a bus, never found his head.

Crowds of families stretched around the gates of the sports fields. White tents with flags atop them, the tricolor of green, white, and gold, and the brewery flag with 1759 written on it. The smell of the fresh-cut grass, white-lined into lanes for running, competition trophies that glinted in the sun.

That day, everything was free. Sweets. Lemonade. Cream buns. Chocolate logs. Ice pops. Popcorn, sweetened and buttered, HB ice cream with wafers. There was free porter for the men, Babycham with bubbles in small glasses for the ladies.

In one tent, there was a rifle gallery, where you squinted one-eyed along the barrel, like in the films, and shot bullets made of cork. If you hit the bull's-eye you won a teddy bear. In another, a distorting mirror made you a long-legged, withery-armed fathead, teeth as big as gravestones when you laughed. We rode like movie cowboys on painted horses, turned in our saddles to shoot at each other with gun-fingers. There was a fancy-dress competition and egg-and-spoon races and a donkey derby.

Men rolled up their sleeves to reveal muscles and tattoos, spat on their hands, and lined up to test their strength on the strongman. When the ball hit the top, everyone cheered.

—Good man yourself there, Tarzan.

In the swinging boat a boy got sick and sprayed the crowd with vomit. On the Ferris wheel, devil-may-care boys blew imaginary smoke out of licorice cigarettes.

I can see our house!
I can see England!

The chairoplanes, with screeching girls pushing their skirts down against the sinful wind. Children got lost and loudspeakers told parents to collect them in the refreshment tent. Rebuke and chocolate cake for being found. Bewildered babies in bonnets told to say cheese for the camera.

—Guess the weight of the turkey and the bird is yours, missus.

—It's a fine fat yoke from the county Wexford.

—Get your free raffle tickets!

—Dinner for two in the Shelbourne Hotel.

—Come on. Let's go in the tunnel of love.

—You can go by yourself, you big eejit. I'll die with the laughing, so I will.

Later, adults jived to the spangle-suited band.

O, let's twist again, like we did last summer.

How to contain the minutes, the hours, the seconds, to make them last forever? Like trying to empty the Irish Sea with a fork.

We sat in the now darkening evening, sun flattened down behind the horizon, painted horses sleeping, swingboats chained, Punch and Judy friends again.

The crowd thinned out on the litter-strewn grass and the air began to chill as cardigans and jumpers were forced over sleepy heads. We trooped out along the gravel pathway, looking back at the lights of the fairground being switched off one by one, until it was in darkness.

—When will the next one be? asked my brother. Because I can't wait to go again. It was the best day of my life, he said.

Father smiled to himself.

—We will all be long gone, dead and buried by the time the next one comes.

As we trudged up the hill, back to our ordinary life, I thought about my father's words and, in my child's mind, the notion of a thing called time.

❧

—Now that you're seven, the nun warned us, you have reached the age of reason. It means you know what you're doing and why, and so it's time to make your first holy communion. You are going to receive a most special sacrament of the Church. A day so special, boys, she said, that a saint girl in the old days died thinking about the excitement of it, the poor creature. God has been thinking about your communion day for all eternity—even as He was making the birds and the animals and the sea and the earth and the sky. Even when He was a baby lying there in the stable in Bethlehem, she continued, He was thinking about the first communion day of all the boys and girls in the world.

I remember feeling ashamed that all I could think of is how much money I would get from our neighbors and relatives.

For this most special day, I had to wear special new clothes. Mother had saved up, putting coins into the mouth of the plastic elephant her brother sent from Texas. I didn't like getting new clothes. It reminded me of when she made me enter a fancy-dress competition as Abraham Lincoln. I'd wanted to go as Roy Rogers, the famous cowboy. She made Lincoln's costume for me, hunched over the sewing machine in the kitchen, needle whirring, leg working the metal plate below.

—Why do I have to go as him?

—Because he's a great American hero.

—So is Roy Rogers.

—He's only a pretend cowboy out of the films.

—Well, Abraham Lincoln couldn't make his horse stand up on its two back legs.

She wedged me into a hat she called a stovepipe that made my ears stick out. The blood throbbed in my head with the tightness of it. People laughed, and I came last.

We practiced our communion with the nuns, who pretended to be the priest as they fed us little bits of plain biscuit as the make-believe body of Christ.

—This is my body, this is my blood, said the nun in a whispery voice. We were warned about touching it with our teeth because the real wafer on communion day would contain God's body as well as His blood.

I left the altar rail and walked down the aisle with a very holy face on me and I knelt there and wondered how God got into a wafer biscuit and where did He go when He was swallowed inside a boy and if He came out in your number two.

Mother was going to take me to the most famous shop in all Ireland, where women from rich parts of the city and wealthy farmers' wives from the country went to shop. But first, we would go to the Shelbourne Hotel.

In the hushed cafe among the pillars and paintings, carpets and comfy sofas, she stirred tea in a china cup with a little silver spoon. Her voice changed to la-di-da when she ordered from the waitress.

—I wonder could we get a fresh pot, like a good girl, this is after going a little cool. Oh, and some strawberry jam if you have it? And a tray of those lovely scones on the trolley. If you wouldn't mind. Thanks ever so, dear.

—O, this is the life, she said, looking around. Stuck in the house from one end of the year to another would put years on a body, she said. Women are hewers of wood and drawers of water and a willing horse gets a heavy load. I want you to make something of yourself in life, learn your books and be a good scholar.

On a raised ledge a lady played the harp, her legs dangling from a chair. Another played the piano, hands hopping along the keys as if they were hot.

—O, Lord, Mother said, the old songs. She loved the songs from the olden days. Now, it's all I can do not to cry listening to John McCormack singing "Oft in the Stilly Night" or "Gortnamona," which she used to sing to herself.

She dabbed at my mouth with her spit on a lipstick-stained handkerchief.

—Oh, I could stay here forever. Wouldn't that be the life. To live in the Shelbourne being waited on hand and foot. Them all at your beck and call.

She asked for the bill and the waitress called her madame.

Afterward we dawdled, looking in shop windows, and strolled down Grafton Street by Trinity College.

> *O Dublin can be heaven*
> *With coffee at eleven*
> *And a stroll in Stephen's Green.*

Then onto Westmoreland Street, over the Liffey and along O'Connell Street until we entered the revolving doors beneath the clock of Clerys department store.

A man in a red uniform held the door of the lift. A chandelier swayed gently as we ascended in a fragrance of wood polish. My mother looked at herself and ran her tongue over her teeth. We reached the second floor, boys and juveniles, and stopped with a small bump.

A greyhound-faced man made sucking sounds through his teeth and measured me from head to toe. Told me to stand straight and ran his hand down my chest. I thought, *This is what a horse must feel like, having bridles and saddles put on, and why they stomp and snort.* The communion blazer itched my neck, and the man stood behind me, in the mirror, moving me this way and that. He brought out patent leather shoes in a box. They looked like girls' Irish dancing shoes, lying there in thin paper, facing each other with white ankle socks beside them. The sucking man bent down, and I could see white scales of skin and red marks in his scalp. He tied the laces in a bow and stood back up with a groan.

—And what about a nice little pair of trousers for the gossoon? the man said. Go in there and take off your clothes.

My own clothes seemed so old and pitiful compared to the new ones. I couldn't even look at my faded vest and underpants in the mirror.

Mother usually dressed us from the secondhand shops in Francis Street. The women there riffled among heaps of clothes and the dealers called out:

—Great bargains, missus, grand little overcoat for the young lad!

—Not a brack on it.

—Hardly ever worn.

I remembered standing in what looked like ladies' bloomers and feeling shame that we couldn't be dressed like other children from real shops. *These clothes are for paupers*, I thought, *alive with fleas, full of holes, always too big or too small.* I watched my mother fumigate those castoffs, which I wore to school, but I had to be slapped into them as she reminded me how grateful I should be to have clothes on my back.

A wave of angry shame came over me as I stood in the cubicle and thought of home. Torn linoleum, overcoats to cover beds, unpapered walls, and cold rooms in winter. My mother's homemade brown bread, not sliced white pan from the shop like the other boys had. When we went on school hikes into the mountains, I pretended I didn't like bread, and threw away the rough brown slices so the other boys wouldn't see.

As a treat sometimes, we would have a family feast and get chips from the chipper with loads of salt and vinegar and toast bread at the fire, holding it over the flames with a straightened-out coat hanger. Before we went to bed Mother would make goody, which is bread mashed in milk and sugar.

> *I know what the baby wants*
> *I know what the baby wants*
> *Goody on a saucer*
> *Goody on a saucer.*

I came out from behind the curtain and my cheeks burned.
—All the girls will be mad about you in that rig-out, the words whistled through his teeth. He folded and parceled up the clothes in brown paper and snipped the twine with scissors. Mother opened her purse and counted out notes followed by a small bag of coins, one by one down on the counter. I looked away, ashamed. I thought what my life would be if I had been an orphan or a mistake.

Or maybe a runaway, leaving one night when they were asleep, up the mountain road and into the pine forest where I'd live on wild berries and rabbits and mushrooms and pass by without them ever knowing. That would serve them all right.

Or dead. I often thought about being dead. That would show them all, crying and weeping and me looking down at them from the sky standing by my grave, sorry that they had treated me so badly.

On the day of my First Communion, I stood with my mother in the garden. Somebody took our photograph. My father had clipped the hedge and it dripped with recent rain, and the curtains of the house had been newly washed and ironed. My mother wore white gloves that came up to her elbows and a small visor with feathers. Her skirt was pleated like the folds of an accordion, and I stood beside her dressed in my new clothes, my cap with the badge of the convent, my green tie, and in my hand my book of prayer with its plastic cover, Jesus looking heavenward. In the rosette on my lapel was the medal of the Holy Ghost. My mother's arm was on my shoulder, she smiled with pride and all my pockets bulged with coins, loaded with money from aunts, uncles, neighbors, even strangers. More money than I'd ever seen.

All that day, I ate every kind of sweet and cake, chocolate and ice cream, gorging on it until the food came up my throat and I forced it back down with lemonade. I was coming to the end of our street when I felt my insides begin to loosen. I made it to Delaney's garden before my bowels erupted. This was where my mother found me. Under the hedge in the darkness, too mortified to move. She covered me with her coat and walked me home saying comforting words, not blaming me at all.

At the Galway Film Festival, one of my first British films, *Defense of the Realm*, had just come out and it was a big success.

I was doing a public interview at the festival when questions from the audience were invited.

A hand was raised. To my horror I realized it was my mother.

—Tell them about when you got diarrhea on your First Communion day. O Lord, she said, that's a good story.

The audience laughed and whooped and applauded. It seems no matter how old you get, your mother will always relish the chance to embarrass you in public.

❧

In 1997, Gianni Versace sent me a note saying that he wanted to dress Leonardo DiCaprio and me for his Paris fashion show.

We had been in the city for four months filming *The Man in the Iron Mask*. Leo was like a little brother, full of mischief and fun. He would come to my trailer to smoke when his mother was on set because she disapproved of his smoking. He had become so famous that girls would run after him in the street, screaming and calling his name. His anonymity and privacy were long gone.

At a suite in the Ritz, Gianni entered holding his poodle, followed by a tailor and a young assistant. He looked like a Roman emperor, with his aquiline nose and silver hair. The dog was asleep in his arms.

His clothes were world-famous. Elton John had donned his frilly lingerie, Sting and his wife Trudie wore his wedding clothes, Elizabeth Hurley's black dress held together with safety pins was infamous. Celebrities lusted for his haute couture, his clinging gold-mesh backless beaded dresses that said, *Look at me. I am glamorous. I am sexy.*

The tailor took my measurements, called out numbers to the assistant, who wrote them in a notebook. Gianni kissed me on both cheeks, said something in Italian, and swept out, the air perfumed in his wake.

On the night of the show we sat, exquisitely attired, at his table. My suit was grey checked, Leo's was dark pinstripe. The gilded room pulsed with wealth and power and sex.

Gianni seemed preoccupied.

—I am so tired, he said. He received compliments with weary grace. I will go in Miami to my house. Escape the people.

The show was a huge success. There was prolonged applause as he stood with his long-legged models, bone-hipped creatures who reminded me of flamingos.

Naomi, dripping in jewels, draped herself over him, left a lipstick stain on his cheek. The film star seated beside me whispered:

—I'm such a silly billy girl. I forgot to put on my underwear.

Jaysus, I thought, *how is that possible*. But I didn't say anything.

Gianni said good night, rough stubble against my cheek.

—*Buona notte, tutti.*

—*Buona notte, maestro*, replied the actress with no underwear.

> *Look at the skies*
> *They've got stars in their eyes*
> *On this lovely bella notte.*

Two days later he was murdered on the steps of his house in Miami by a twenty-seven-year-old psychopath who later killed himself with the same gun.

They found a list of potential victims in his pocket. Among the names was Leo's.

I thought of Gianni bowing that night and then murdered, lying alone in a pool of blood on the steps of his house, having just returned from breakfast at his favorite cafe.

His sister Donatella said he died like an emperor. Facing
the sky.

∿⨀⊙⨀∿

Like many Irish children, I made my acting debut in a nativ-
ity play. Goose Gavin with jug-handle ears and a big, red face
landed the role of St. Joseph. Burkey, who had fleas that jumped
out from under his collar, was Mary, dressed in a blue curtain.
The baby Jesus was a rubber doll. There were angels and wise
men who came from the East with nice presents.

The Virgin Mary said to the wise men:

—Youse shouldn't have gone to all that trouble, youse—

—Not YOUSE!!! the nun shouted. *Youse* is what common
people say. The holy family aren't from the tenements.

—How did you find out where we were? said Joseph to the
three wise men.

—A star appeared in the east and we just kept following it.

—That was an awful long way to walk.

—We came on camels, but we had to leave them outside.

The nun made them say that because there wasn't enough
material to make three camel costumes.

I was given the part of a shepherd and was dressed in a white
sheet with a stick for my staff. I had a beard made from cotton
wool, which the nun glued to my face. I sat on a shepherd's rock,
which was a biscuit tin covered in silver paper. I had to pretend I
was on a hill in Bethlehem and not outside the window where the
toilets were. A boy made *baa-baaa* sounds behind the curtains so
that everyone would think he was really a sheep.

The night of the play the hall filled with our families.
Their clapping sounded like rain on a roof. The three wise men
together asked me:

—By any chance are we on the right road for Bethlehem? and my beard fell off and was kicked into a woman's lap in the front row by the holy family's donkey, which the Grealish twins were inside of.

She handed it back and I held it to my face.

Mary asked the innkeeper:

—Do you have any room for the holy family? I'm heavy with child.

—There is only a stable out the back with all straw in it. The hotels are full up because it's a very busy time of the year.

—Don't worry, Mary, said St. Joseph, I will make it nice and cozy for us.

—Are you sure, Joseph? It's very cold.

—The animals will keep us warm by breathing on us, Mary. Then the animals and the humans sang "Away in a Manger."

The lights went out and when they came on again, the Virgin Mary was giving the baby Jesus his bottle. The manger was crowded with sheep and cows, and wise men and the donkey.

—I have bad news, the angel said and looked at me strangely. I glanced down and saw piss coming like a snake from the angel toward me, then flowing under my shepherd's sandals. There is an evil king who's going to kill all the little babies in Israel, so baby Jesus, Mary, and Joseph have to fly into Egypt.

So, the holy family put the rubber doll up on the donkey's back and Goose Gavin said:

—Thanks for everything. Goodbye now.

We all waved goodbye to the holy family, and that was the end of the play.

We bowed, and all the grown-ups clapped and cheered. We got Toblerone chocolate and lemonade as a special treat. The nun was kind now, because she was proud, and we were happy to have pleased her and made her smile.

But I was sad the play was over. I just wanted to do it all over again. It was like waking from a lovely dream. She said maybe next year I could be St. Joseph, and I ran into the yard leapfrogging and chasing and rolling in the grass, so excited with all the praise we got.

—Who made your beard? You'd swear it was real, said Goose Gavin's father, winking and laughing. He had the same red face and jug-handle ears as Goosey. All the grown-ups laughed too, and nobody said anything about it falling off, or the angel going to the toilet all over the floor, or the cow having a common accent from the tenements.

Mother and Father were proud of me. Their praise felt warm inside me. They took me to the zoo for a reward, and Mother had her photograph taken in her brown-and-white-spotted frock in front of the giraffe. And I walked between Father and Mother like the holy family, happy in the livelong day that we didn't have to fly into Egypt to escape from Herod.

I'VE WORKED IN MY FILM CAREER with some of cinema's great directors. But that nun was my first director in that little play.

Many years later, John Boorman, the world-renowned director of *Deliverance* and *Point Blank*, came to see me in a play. He offered me a leading role in a film he was going to shoot in Ireland called *Excalibur*. It was the biggest production there since David Lean made *Ryan's Daughter*.

This would be the first film role of my career.

I knew nothing about the technicalities of working in front of a camera, although I had a little experience of television.

We rehearsed in London and the first morning of the read-through I got on the wrong bus and arrived an hour late to face a table of esteemed actors. And John Boorman.

Nobody paid much attention to me and they had already gone past my role. I sat down sweating and mortified.

Like every actor in Dublin I had lied when I was asked if I could ride a horse. Essential in a film about Arthurian knights. Myself and several other liars were cast.

I was dispatched to Hyde Park to take lessons from a floppy-haired youth in skintight dung-stained riding britches. He warned me not to gallop, as a rider had been fined for speeding by the police.

Also would I mind if an American lady joined me?

We were given clumpy horses and told to be back in an hour. He went on raking dung.

We ambled around the park. The American was a beautiful older woman with startling eyes and a full mouth. She swore a lot. I liked her immediately. She had a fine throaty laugh as if she'd smoked lots of cigarettes.

She was living in London. She loved its architecture and the people and felt really at home there. I told her the name of the film I was making. She said that sounded interesting. She liked to cook and visit the theater. She asked me what kind of horse I would be riding.

—A polo pony? Shouldn't you be taking lessons on the real thing? They are notoriously fast and respond to just a finger on the reins.

—I'm breaking myself in gradually.

—Well, I hope these nags get us back to base, she said.

I admired her red slippers, which looked so delicate in the stirrups.

—I never wore shoes when I was a kid growing up, she said.

Back at the stable, the floppy-haired youth took my horse.

—How did you like Ava? he asked.

—Ava? I said.

—That was Ava Gardner you were riding with.

We had sword-fighting lessons. The swords were heavy and unwieldy.

—John wants the real thing, said the fight trainer. No Errol Flynn bollocks. And the armor will be real and heavy. You'll be walking and riding like they used to walk and ride in those days.

It took twenty minutes to get into the gear. I was given a helmet with a kind of snout in front. I felt like I was looking out of a postbox, clanking and falling over like a tortoise unable to right itself.

—Now comes the good bit, said the horse master. You have to ride in armor.

We were hoisted onto the backs of the polo ponies and they took off faster than a racing car as we were bounced up and down, terrified inside. My gloves were made of some kind of iron. My feet were out of the stirrups and wind whistled through my helmet's snout as I flew through the air and landed in a swamp. The sky above, the mud below. The movies.

However, we improved day by day and eventually we became devil-may-care, but we still complained about being trapped inside our armor. Relieving ourselves required such effort to dismount, so clouds of steam would issue forth as an actor went cross-eyed with relief. Now we complained about leg rash.

I found it difficult to master the technique of acting for the film camera. In the theater we went on and kept going till the curtain fell. Here we were stopped constantly for so many reasons, from the sun going behind clouds to other things beyond my knowledge.

My character was a fearsome warlord who steals the wife of a nobleman and takes her against her will in a suit of armor with no egress.

—How do I, you know, do the, em, business? I said to John Boorman.

—Just fake it, he said. We're mostly on faces except for the wide shot. I had no idea what that meant. But was too nervous to ask.

The scene took place in front of a roaring fire. The actress lay beneath me.

—Good for the wide. Let's go closer, said John. The actress was removed and replaced by a pink cushion.

—Excuse me, I said to the cinematographer, why is there a cushion here?

—To make the humping more real, he said, looking through a black eyeglass.

Sweating in full armor before the ferocious fire, I gave it to the cushion for eleven takes before I collapsed exhausted.

John was a hard taskmaster and we were very respectful but wary of him.

One day early on, all the knights were gathered around a table, bearded and roaring and iron-gloved, when there was a sudden silence. A man with two huge dogs was making his way off set, lugging them with chains.

Boorman's face was dark.

—He's fired the fucking dogs. Keep your head down or we'll be next.

I had to wade through a field of mud, red-eyed and black-faced from the burning tractor tires set on fire to simulate the smoke of battle.

I was carrying the great sword Excalibur to plunge it into the stone which was made of polystyrene and fake moss. For whosoever wrested the great sword from it would be the rightful king.

The sound of the sword plunging into that thing went through me like the proverbial fingernails on a blackboard.

—Why are you grimacing? John said.

—I can't do it. I don't like the sound it's making.

—You are a mythological prehistoric brute who has just staggered twenty miles across a swamp. This is a climactic moment in the story and you're telling me you don't like the sound? And his face began to take on the same look as when he fired the two mastiffs.

Back to first positions.

I was learning fast the techniques of acting for the screen.

At the premiere many moments received applause. Not least the ear-shattering insertion of the sword into the ancient stone, enhanced now with brilliant sound effects. But loudest of all was when my character humped in a full suit of armor.

〜◦⟋⟍◦〜

Over drinks, a producer friend had thrown down a script the size of a telephone directory. "Wagner," it read.

—Any role you like! Except Wagner himself obviously. Richard will be playing the old boy.

—I think the role of Liszt would be up my alley . . .

—That's going to be Ekkehard Schall from the Berliner Ensemble, the son-in-law of Brecht and all that. We're shooting some parts in Germany and they're putting in some dosh, so we have to give one of theirs a big bone.

I called the following day.

—Richter the composer?

—We've promised it to the Austrians. That's the problem, you see, with Euro puddings. Each country has to have a slice.

—What about Karl Ritter? He doesn't say much but he shows up in every location.

My girlfriend Aine and I had been in London for eighteen months and, apart from a play at the BBC, I had been unemployed and on welfare for seventeen months. I had begun to accept that I might never work anywhere again. We had taken a risk and left my theatrical success in Dublin behind. It was a turbulent time politically. Rupert Murdoch was destroying unions and Margaret Thatcher was taking away free milk from schoolchildren, privatizing and deregulating, favoring the elite, punishing the poor through austerity, while she invaded the Falklands.

The IRA had resumed its campaign on the mainland, and anti-Irish feeling was everywhere. I was careful about speaking with my accent, and in auditions I was constantly asked if I could change it. I was told I needed to learn to speak like an English actor if I was ever to get work and progress beyond roles of wily peasants and bombers.

Ritter, patron of Wagner, for whom the composer had utter disdain, was a rich dilettante. It wasn't much of a part, his primary dramatic function being to incite the great man to insult.

RITTER: [stuttering] *Herr Wagner I . . .*
WAGNER: [losing his temper] *O be quiet Ritter, you fool!*
RITTER: [spluttering] *But Herr Wagner . . .*
WAGNER: *Get out of my sight.*

RITTER exits crestfallen.

WAGNER: [to actor with very big role] *How I detest that idiot.*

It was money and we were broke. And I would be working with some of the greatest stars in the world: Burton, Richardson, Olivier, Gielgud, and Redgrave. Or at least I'd get to watch them work. I had ten lines in six countries.

In my research I could find little to nothing on Herr Ritter so I took dramatic license and decided on a pince-nez and a thin mustache to give him character. Nothing in the script indicated that Herr Ritter was anything more than a device to propel the plot. He could have been replaced by stage directions.

—Are you sure the mustache is a good idea? You can't grow one. It'll have to be fake. With glue and all. You know how you are with things like that, Aine said.

I collected my welfare money on Friday as usual, and took rent to our landlord, a plump man with ginger mutton chops. He was some class of accountant in real life with dodgy rental properties on the side. I was craven in my dealings with him, as we lived under constant threat of eviction.

Afterward, I went to the pub and was smoking a cigarette with my friend Reggie, an old bookseller. Mrs. Thatcher was on the television, glorifying her bloodlust, crowing about democracy.

—That fuckin' witch. I cannot stand her voice, he said.

A poll in one of the tabloids announced she had been voted the sexiest woman in Britain.

—Yeah, said Reggie, if you like a good lash of the cane across the arse and being sent to the nursery with no supper.

Then Aine burst into the pub to tell me, breathlessly, that I had to leave at once for the airport!

—For Venice! This afternoon! Venice, Italy!

There had been a change in the shooting schedule and a car would collect me in an hour. We rushed back to the flat, threw some clothes into a plastic bag (having pawned the suitcases we'd left Ireland with), and I hightailed it to Heathrow in a manky minicab.

I was so unused to being on a plane that I took photographs of the wing.

Three hours later I was in a motorboat speeding toward Venice and then I was on a balcony at the Gritti Palace Hotel on the Grand Canal, in a suite no less. I had never stayed in such luxury before. Beautifully appointed gilded rooms, crystal chandeliers, silk coverlets, mint chocolates on the starched white pillowcases, Chopin nocturnes issuing from the bedside radio. On the table rested a bowl of fruit and a bottle of vintage champagne welcoming me to the hotel. How thrilled they were to have me there. How excited they were to be working with me.

—Well, fuck yeah! This is a bit more like it, boys!

I opened the long windows and the lightly-scented evening breeze drifted into the room. Over the canal, the sky changed from blue to grey and red in the dying sun. Lovers lounged in gondolas rowed by men in black hats and striped shirts, just like on the television. Laughter echoed off the walls of houses, footsteps loud in the alleyways.

I wandered around the suite, too restless to settle.

I opened one of the ornate cupboards. It was a fridge stocked with rows of miniature drinks.

Regret came over me for Aine and the decrepit flat I'd left her with, its threadbare carpets and plywood partitions. She would have shared my restless excitement, but we couldn't afford a second ticket.

I opened a bottle of brandy, poured myself a measure, and took some of the fire out with a slap of champagne. Then I sauntered onto the balcony, drew up a silk chair, lit a cigarette, and waved languidly at the passing boats.

—You must be Ritter. Behind me from the other balcony, a large glass of amber in his hand, Burton and his unmistakable voice.

—Jaysus. Mr. Burton.

—Richard, he said.

The following day, an explosion of cameras flashed on the quayside. Photographers from all over the world jostled each other to capture his every move. They fell over each other and one across the bonnet of a moving car.

So this is what fame looks like, I thought, as they almost crushed him.

—Richard! they shouted. This way! Look here, Rich.

—Is it true you're getting back with Liz?

He was helped coughing and bleary-eyed into the gondola where I sat nervously waiting to rehearse our scene. Ekkehard Schall as Liszt in black looked like a bad-tempered nun.

My false mustache itched my lips, and the spectacles with real lenses made me dizzy and disorientated and had the effect of fuzzing everything. I was beginning to feel nauseous but was too nervous to say anything. My costume was a beautifully tailored suit of black over a starched white shirt. I also wore a silk top hat.

We were punted away from the main canal to a quiet place with no crowds. A larger boat drew up alongside with the director, camera crew, makeup, hair, and technicians aboard.

Many voices, all shouting over each other, reverberated in my skull. There was also the dim memory of a drunken phone call to Aine from the hotel phone which I feared would take care of my entire fee for the job. My head throbbed. My tongue rough as the floor of a budgie's cage.

I was the rower of the boat but the oars were slapping the water unevenly, creaking in their handles, flailing the air wildly.

—You've got to get the oars going at the same time, shouted a megaphone.

I felt as if I was at school again standing in front of a class being asked to solve some idiotic problem about men in a hole digging at a rate of two feet an hour if the square on the hypotenuse equals the bishop of Cork. My old demon mates, doubt, fear, and shame, were now sitting in the boat as well. My mustache had begun to itch more violently and was now detaching itself from my lip. I tried to push it back into place with my tongue but only succeeded in sucking it into my mouth. Liszt was staring at me.

—He iss eatink hiss whiskiss, he said like a telltale to the director in the crew boat.

I removed the caterpillar of mustache from my tongue.

—Jesus Christ! barked the assistant director, where's makeup?

A nervous girl was lowered gingerly into the boat, clutching a little bag of brushes tightly to her.

I stood up.

—Sit the fuck down, barked the megaphone. Let her come to you.

I sat down. She extracted her scissors and began to snip delicately. In silence the entire crew watched. The producer looked impatiently at his watch.

Suddenly a rogue wave rolled under the boat. The swell unbalanced the makeup artist, and the blade of her scissors went through my lip. Within moments blood was dripping onto my starched white shirt.

—Jesus H. Christ! Get them up here! Get the nurse! shouted the megaphone. I was led ignominiously up the gangplank. The nurse applied iodine and a bandage and I was dismissed for the day.

I returned to my suite and attacked the minibar again, although it was still midmorning. I watched *Brief Encounter*, dubbed in Italian, and sucked brandy through a straw, my lip throbbing. Sometime that evening the phone awoke me from my coma.

—Hello Lippy, said Burton. Come and have a drink.

We sat on his terrace, me with my bandaged lip, drinking late into the evening until I felt at ease and drunk again, realizing that the shame of a split lip was nothing when you thought about it, especially if it meant you could spend time in the company of your hero, his voice directed at you alone. One of the world's greatest actors. I'd been watching his performances in the picture houses of Dublin for years, and now here I was getting drunk with him. I remarked on the chaos of the photographers that morning.

—Fame, Burton said, doesn't change who you are, it changes others. It is a sweet poison you drink of first in eager gulps. Then you come to loathe it.

I'm rather ashamed to be an actor sometimes. I've done the most appalling shit for money.

I detest the self mirrored back to me by others. It's a kind of fractured reality. I can't see me.

But this Jameson's makes sense of everything, for the moment. And poetry, the sound and music of words sooth me, always have. And books.

Home is where the books are, he said.

What I've always rather wanted was to be a writer, perhaps it's too late now.

I am at an age, he said quietly, when I fear dying in a hotel room on a film.

How's your lip? he asked, as we bade good night at the door.

—I think Doctor Jameson has me sorted, I said.

—Give it all you've got but never forget it's just a bloody movie, that's all it is. We're not curing cancer. Remember.

I've made over eighty films since then and I've never forgotten those words.

He didn't die in a hotel room but at home in bed, halfway through a volume of the Elizabethan poets.

~❦~

The company moved on to Vienna, where we saw one of Nureyev's last performances.

His face was a mask of cold passion and arrogance. How bitter to drink the last dregs of fame Burton despised, knowing the audience was judging him now with pity and the memories of his greater triumphs.

The scenes with the three great knights of the English theatre, Gielgud, Olivier, and Richardson, were to be filmed on location there, a historic moment as they had never appeared together on stage or film.

One afternoon in the corridor of the studio, I saw an elderly man come out of the star dressing room.

He started to pace up and down, talking to himself. As I drew near I realized it was one of the great knights, and my other hero, Sir Laurence Olivier. He glanced crossly at me.

What should I say? It's a real honor to meet you, sir. I have long been an admirer of yours.

I heard myself say:

—Excuse me, do you have the time?

Heathcliff, Maxim de Winter, and Hamlet all glared at me.

—Are they paying you on this thing?

I stammered that they were.

—Then you should buy yourself a watch. And he continued down the corridor talking to himself.

On the day of Gielgud, Olivier, and Richardson's scene, the location, an old convent, was packed with extras and thrilled onlookers. The knights were playing high-ranking officers in the Prussian army.

Gielgud had told us he was so old he liked to pretend to die in the middle of a scene just to keep the producers on their toes.

Midway through the first take Olivier stopped and called the director to him. After some moments of hushed consultation, the megaphone was lifted.

—Get wardrobe!

He had noticed that the epaulets of his uniform indicated a lesser rank than the other two. And had made it known with ingratiating humility.

Respectfully, and patiently, production waited for the costumers to arrive and promote him to equal rank.

Everyone knew that despite all the acclaim he was still and always had been extremely competitive.

I'd heard a story about him and Rex Harrison as young men. In London in the twenties they had been rivals, envious and resentful of one another's talent. Rex was the light comedian, Larry, the tragedian. The rivalry had lasted all their lives, each wishing they had the career of the other. Until one day at the Midland Hotel in Manchester, Olivier, who was playing Lear for television, now old and stooped with white beard and hair, was in the elevator. The lift stopped and in walked another old gent, also white-haired and bearded. It was Rex Harrison. They didn't recognize each other.

I was disappointed my only interaction with Olivier had been my stupid question about the time.

The three knights departed.

My dressing room was no larger than a wardrobe, so I spent little time there except to sleep.

I almost didn't see the small envelope addressed to me leaning against the mirror. Inside was a note from him.

> *Apologies old chap if I appeared rather brusque when we met. I was attempting to knock my lines into my stupid old head.*
>
> *I've thought about your question regarding the time.*
>
> *It's something I think about a great deal these days. And in reply please allow a greater mind than I to answer.*

And there followed Shakespeare's Sonnet 60, written in neat black cursive. He had underlined the following lines.

> *Like as the waves make towards the pebbled shore,*
> *So do our minutes hasten to their end . . .*

And Time, that gave, doth now his gift confound.
Time doth transfix the flourish set on youth,
And delves the parallels in beauty's brow,
Feeds on the rarities of nature's truth,
And nothing stands but for his scythe to mow.

Affectionately
Larry.

AS A CHILD, I was always fearful, frightened by so many things. The lights of a car shining through the branches of a tree at night, its shadows sweeping across my bedroom, could terrify me. I would lie awake for hours listening for the footsteps of kidnappers and murderers on the stair, until finally worn out I would fall into sleep. Morning light defined the room slowly and all was reassuring again. I would laugh at my cowardly custard self.

On bleak winter evenings, home from school, I would set the fire with paper and slack and bits of sticks gathered from fallen branches in the garden and, finally, some sugar sprinkled over to give it flame. I was a good fire-maker. I like to watch the flames' reflection in the windowpane, as if they were burning outside in the garden. The fire comforted me and took the fear out of the evening. Since then I've never lived in a house that didn't have a fireplace.

Every fortnight my mother would take me on the bus to see an old lady called Mrs. Gordon who lived on Northumberland Road, a street near the canal. She had been a patient of my mother's at the hospital years before. Mrs. Gordon had a maid called Molly, who would take our coats and bring me to the kitchen and feed me scones and hot milk.

Molly would ask what I was going to be when I grew up and whether I liked school and did I have a little sweetheart yet. She would complain about Mrs. Gordon.

—God forgive me but she can be an old pill the way she does have me always at her beck and call. I'm run off my feet so I am.

She would walk me upstairs to the room where my mother and the old lady sat, and Molly would make up to her, sweet as pie, fluffing her cushions.

—Are you comfortable there, Mrs. G.? Would you like a blanket? Will I put a bit of slack on that fire for you? Maybe a nice little sup of sherry, Mrs. G.?

The old lady would make me sit opposite her. Her hands reminded me of greaseproof paper, covered with knobbly purple veins. She always wore black, and a locket at her throat that held hairs from her dead husband's mustache inside. She also wore an eyepatch under her glasses and her other eye rolled around like a big marble. Ash from her cigarette would drop onto her dress and the cat in her lap. Sometimes she would open her legs and I would see up to her knickers. There was a smell off her, which Molly told me was because Mrs. G. didn't wash herself except for the odd time when the doctor came.

Around the room, stuffed dead birds in glass cases stared at me. On the wall hung photographs of Mrs. G. when she was young sitting in a chair with her husband's hand on her shoulder.

—A pure gentleman he was, Molly said, always dressed to the nines, shoes polished like chestnuts you could see your-self in. Went off very sudden in the end, the heart. Left all to herself above. She never remarried and stayed a widdy woman to this day.

During these visits, I would hold my toilet until I could bear it no longer. I was afraid of the cold musty bathroom at the top of the dark staircase.

Mrs. G. had lived in her house since childhood. She told me about the time in April 1921 when there was a battle between the British Army and Irish soldiers outside the house.

—Myself and Mother and my sisters were terrified, with the bullets whistling and cracking for three days. When it was over, there was blood all over the streets, soldiers and innocent people lying dead or wounded, groaning on the steps of houses and gardens. What was it all for in the end, the fighting and dying, families destroyed with the grief? Brother fighting brother.

She pointed her stick down at the road where lamps shone and cars and buses passed. She told stories of the Black and Tans, who were a reserve force of British soldiers.

—Oh I'll never forget them. You'd hear them coming in their Crossly Tender trucks, firing at people just for fun or jeering at them walking the roads. Mad drunk. The most awful language out of them. They were the dregs out of mental hospitals and prisons, most of them. They had no respect for man nor beast. When we'd hear them we'd hide because they'd shoot you soon as look at you. I'll never forget the day they burst into the chapel and shouted at the priest to get off the altar and fired their bullets into the roof and at the stained glass windows. The poor old parish priest faced them down, told them to have respect for the house of God.

—Shut up, vicar, they said, and knocked him to the ground. They said they were looking for rebels.

Mother had heard a story that they'd taken two boys, tied them to the back of one of their trucks, and dragged them along the roads till there was nothing but two bloody lumps dumped in the village as a warning. Her mother had told her of her grandmother's memories of people skeletal by the roadside, mouths green from eating grass during the famine days when half of Ireland starved to death because the potatoes went rotten and black in the ground as the remaining food was shipped to England under armed guard.

Mrs. Gordon told me stories of giants who had gone to sleep in the sea, where trees grew over them and they became islands. Of towns underwater where phantom bells still rang and cattle lowed. The old people when she was a child believed in other worlds beyond what we can see with human eyes, in fairies that could steal a child away in the night from a crib and replace it with a sickly thing which would waste away and die.

—There was a girl the old people used to talk about who had been taken by the fairies, and she was gone many a year and the parents had given up hope of ever seeing her again. Then one day at a fair, didn't they see a woman the spit of their own child, and didn't the woman put her finger to her lips to bid them be silent and to make no move toward her, and she disappeared again away among the crowds. Things like that we cannot explain away.

The fairies thought the mortal world of ours was a cruel place. They were magical and mysterious creatures. They could change shape to become birds or beasts or the wind itself and they were as many and as small as blades of grass in a field. They drank magic wine from the bluebell flower. But they loved a bit of curranty cake with a nice glawb of butter and jam on it. The old people would leave a bottle of stout for them under the hedge and a bit of food so they wouldn't do any harm to a person during the night. They were pure divils for stealing keys and odd shoes and socks from the human world, and they'd hide them underground in their caves where you'd never see them again and not even St. Anthony himself could find them.

Mrs. Gordon said the most frightening thing in the whole world was a fairy woman called the banshee. She followed certain families to warn of death, and if you heard her cries you'd know for sure a death was coming. The banshee was tall and stood beneath a tree, combing her long red hair, and her crying and moaning would freeze the blood in your veins.

—And another creature you wouldn't want to lay eyes on is Dullahan. This lad rode around the country on a black horse and what do you think he was carrying? His own head. And there'd be flames inside the eyes to light his way. He'd pull up outside your house and call your name and that meant your days on this earth were done.

—That's all made-up old stuff, my mother said. Don't pay any heed on it, only rawmaish. That woman should have more sense than to be scaring children. There are more frightening things in the world than fairies and banshees and dullahans, you'll come to see that. But I knew she believed in them deep down.

Like my grandmother with films, Mrs. Gordon opened a door for me to the world. She liked to read newspaper stories to me with a magnifying glass. There was one about a boy who had been raised with hens. He had been in a cage since he was two years old. He had never laid eyes on a human except a woman who came twice a day and fed him out of a basin. The boy didn't know the woman was his mother. One day a neighbor happened to see him. She told the police and they came and let him free. They couldn't believe their eyes the way he was, his elbows going in and out like wings, pecking for food on the ground, and standing on one leg giving little squawks. I couldn't stop thinking about him and how he had to go to school now, and learn stupid things like algebra; how he had to wear shoes, and learn to sit on the pot like a person and not do poo standing up like a hen. I felt sorry for the henhouse boy, and thought if I could be his friend I would take him to the pictures so he'd know that everybody in the world wasn't cruel. We would be best friends and after a while he'd forget he ever believed he was a hen. We would play football with the washing line as the goal, and I'd be Liverpool and the henboy would be Manchester United and I'd let him win. I wondered if the hens missed the boy when they put their heads under their wings to go to sleep at nighttime. But they were hens, Mrs. G. said, so they couldn't understand our human world.

Another story was about a baby girl who was born on a plane and who died just before it landed.

—Isn't it sad she never got baptized and has to go to Limbo. Limbo is like a left-luggage room for babies, all crying to get up to Heaven because they haven't been baptized. They have no mothers to comfort them and they have to wait till Holy God says it's alright for them to come up to Heaven and gaze upon His face for all eternity.

I said a prayer for the baby girl who was alive for only a few hours up there in the sky, so that one day soon, she would get out of Limbo and fly up to Heaven in her nappy with a pair of brand-new wings.

Mrs. G. showed me a photograph of Laika the Russian dog looking out the window of a spaceship. Her face looked sad.

—Does she know she's going to the moon? I asked, as we both stared at her worried eyes. She was blasted into space and everybody thought it was such fun, like the dog that jumped over the moon. Then it was on the radio that the spaceship had exploded and there wasn't a trace left of the sad-faced dog anywhere in the sky or on the earth.

Mrs. G. showed me faces of murdered people staring out of photographs.

—They didn't know when someone said *look at the dickey bird and say cheese* that they'd be in the paper for being murdered.

Pearl in the headscarf walking home from the dance and her body found in a field covered in frost; or a little boy called Tommy who was found strangled in a graveyard.

—Ghosts can be unhappy souls, Mrs. Gordon said, who leave this world too soon.

They were ghosts now, and I wanted them to haunt whoever had killed them and make them confess and go to jail forever. I imagined them wandering the roads, crying silently because of what had been done to them. The restless dead.

I would have the same terrifying dream in which I saw the death coach dragged by four black horses creaking and swaying up the hill to my house; ghosts behind it making a kind of music with the bones and skin of the dead. The Devil, cloven-hoofed, saluting me with a silver cane, his dogs snarling, teeth bared. A faceless woman, her red hair flying wild in the wind, a graveyard bride in her mud-splashed wedding dress, who spent her nights searching among the headstones for her true love. She died of a broken heart.

—People die from such things, Mrs. Gordon said.

The ghosts of my dreams all shuffling along till their crying died away in the night.

—What's Heaven like? I asked her once. Was it full of saints and holy people who went to mass and confession?

—Heaven is a beautiful country out behind the moon, with rivers and trees and fields and sun shining forever and ever. There are sweetshops and ice cream.

I made Mrs. Gordon promise she would never haunt me and she laughed and said that if she was a ghost she'd only be a kind one looking out for me.

∾っⓒ∾ⓒ∾

People were worried that the Russians could invade Ireland.

—They will overrun the world, the priest said from the pulpit.

We prayed in our classroom and in the chapel for the conversion of Red Russia. We were told that Communists hated Catholics worse than Henry the Eighth or Cromwell.

—They believe in no god and if they take over the world, Irish people could all be sent off to the camps of Siberia. Our Lady, Father Burke said, was worried about them too; it makes her heart very heavy and sad that there are so many pagan countries in the world.

—Where would you hide if the Russians come? a boy asked me.

—Maybe in the wild bushes near the river.

—Sure they'd find you there easy as anything, he said.

At my uncle's house in the country, my brothers and sisters and I stood in the crowd with him outside Carney's electrical goods shop and gents' outfitters. In the window, among the sports coats and Hoovers, a television flashed black and white. On its screen, the leaders of the world: Khrushchev the Communist, and Kennedy the Catholic. A man who could read lips, on account of his son being deaf and mute, repeated what they were saying.

—There's going to be a nuclear war between Russia and the Yanks.

At night I couldn't sleep as I thought of all the rivers on fire, even the mountains would be ashes. Lava would pour through the streets and flesh would fall from the bones of everyone I loved.

I remember the dreadful feeling as we stood among silent crowds that lined the streets in sorrow as the funeral of the Irish soldiers who had been murdered in an ambush in the Congo passed by. On the gun carriages were lead caskets wrapped in the flag of Ireland, the soldiers' caps resting atop; the army band played the dead march as the soldiers journeyed to their final resting place at Glasnevin to be buried alongside the heroes of Ireland. The sky had gone black with arrows and poisoned spears. They had been massacred in minutes. That was all we knew of war.

I remember looking at the round blue globe by the door, at the little patch that was Ireland.

—People we don't know and things we don't understand in faraway places decide whether we live or die, my uncle said.

I listened to the grown-ups talking low and gravely among themselves.

—I'd say it's what's in the secret of Fátima. They have it hidden away in a secret room in the Vatican, our Blessed Lady revealed it to the children on the hillside. She told them only to tell the Pope.

—The Yanks should drop a bomb on them like they did on the Japanese.

I remember how then we walked out over the fields to bring home the cattle for milking. I envied the birds who thought nothing about rivers on fire and burned skeletons in the streets.

We stood for a moment looking over the land. My uncle pulled hard on his cigarette and exhaled, the smoke hanging in the still air, and I imagined for a moment it was a nuclear cloud.

The conflict was resolved somehow.

I remember walking up the hill from the town a week later.

The land seemed under a spell of peace. The fields, the river, the birds and animals all seemed to know that we would live.

One day we were out playing when there was a crack of rifle fire.

—Someone out shooting rabbits maybe, was all my uncle said when he saw I was afraid.

There was a holy well among the trees. It had always been there. The steps had been smoothed by centuries of people praying on their knees, and drinking its blessed water from an iron cup chained to a rock. Often they would leave a medal or some precious keepsake on a branch so that their wishes would pass into it.

There was a legend that a golden trout lived in its depths and if you caught sight of it your prayer would be answered. My uncle told us he saw something brown which twisted and gleamed and disappeared. Maybe it was just a trick of sunlight.

I pushed the leaves away with the cup's rim and drank the cold water.

I gave thanks to God and prayed for all the people I loved that there would be no more war.

I've made several films about war and with every character I've played, I've been reminded of my childhood fears, the dreams and nightmares, the imaginings I endured so real sometimes I felt they had really happened.

In 2002, I would find myself in St. Petersburg, working on a film about the siege of Leningrad in World War II.

There was a very old Russian extra with whom I used to talk during breaks. He told me that he too, like all his countrymen, had feared nuclear war. The Russians had been convinced of the inevitability of their own annihilation. But he had fought his own war and it had left deep wounds in his soul, although he had come through safe.

He was having his Polaroid photograph taken for costume continuity. He asked the assistant if she would take one just for him. It whirred out of the little machine. He looked at it for a few moments, then placed it in his inside pocket.

We sat and talked and he told me a story about another photograph. He said the Polaroid reminded him of when he was a partisan fighting the Germans.

—I sat before the window, knapsack at my feet, the old gun of my father loose in my lap. I was looking out at our village like it was for the last time, trying to make each familiar landmark strange so I'd remember it all the more. I'd left my wife in bed. She hadn't slept either. In the darkness, she had woken me trying to stifle her soft crying. I have to go, I told her gently.

The day before, we'd heard the sound of the guns. Like children's firecrackers. A few days before that, the commander of the partisan army in that part of Belorussia himself came with another man to say it was time. If I'm honest I felt a bolt of excitement I'd never felt before. I wanted to go to war, to fight and kill the Germans. Our villages on the edge of forest and swamp had so far escaped the horrors we kept hearing about. It was hard in the peace of that place to imagine that such a world existed. I was a farmer, you see. I worked in the fields from dawn light to dusk.

One day, we were working in the fields when we heard the drone of a plane above, hanging still in the sky, like a hawk, before dropping leaflets. "The German is your friend," it said in our language. Soon they would return with their bombs.

That morning, my wife set milk and bread before me. I touched her hand and she came to me then and we held each other. I know she felt in her heart that I was going to die and that she would never see me again and I felt it too.

The soldiers came in, eyes bloodshot, faces unshaven, and she gave them something to eat and drink. Then it was time to leave.

I kissed my wife again. She gave me a photograph of herself. I put it in my inside pocket.

The women of the village blessed us as the cart rumbled out past the frozen fields. We collected others and traveled onwards for many hours. Beneath the star-filled sky we sang songs of home and it made me so sad I cannot tell you.

That winter was cruel, I can tell you. We marched across the mountains, sleeping wherever we could, living off the land. And when we found them, we showed no mercy. Even when they were young kids and shitting themselves with fear. I pulled the trigger and watched them die. Sometimes we made them beg for the final merciful bullet.

My hair had turned grey, deep lines etched in my face. I couldn't remember how long ago it had been since we'd left. I'd begun to forget I had another life.

Sometimes I'd dream of the pathway leading to my house. I would push open the door and there would only be cobwebs. I'd lost the photograph my wife had given me. So I'd close my eyes and imagine. To remember and imagine can be the same thing.

Once, near the end, we came on a place of blackened bones scattered in the snow, not a sound of animal or man. In the swamp we found a shivering boy who told us what had happened. The Germans had appeared suddenly in trucks. They rounded up the villagers, all the while playing German music from a loudspeaker. Forced them into a building. Locked the doors. Emptied cans of gasoline through the windows and over the roof. They stood there drunk and laughing until the last pitiful cry.

Hearing that story, I couldn't cry. Not a tear. I was dead inside.

Then one day news came that the Germans were in retreat and were defeated. We felt no sense of relief or victory, so numb had our hearts become, you see.

One by one we took our leave of each other and began the slow trek toward home. When I came to the rise at the end of our valley I could see the village below. Moonlight still over the roofs. A light burned here and there, yellow and smudged. I came down that pathway I'd dreamed so often of. I stood on the steps listening for sounds. I heard a movement inside. I dared not knock at the door.

My wife thought she'd heard something outside and was drawn to the window where she had waited every day. Frost covered the glass with flowers. She scraped an opening with her fingernail. And then she saw my face looking at her. She thought she was seeing a ghost and I thought I was dreaming again. We stood there looking at each other. Afraid to speak. Afraid to move.

And we stayed like that for hours until dawn came over the hill.

❧❀❧

The Christian Brothers' School House for Older Boys, where I was sent at age ten, was an old castle from the thirteenth century. It stood in a field, surrounded by a moat in which a boat rotted among the reeds. Oliver Cromwell, the English general, kept his horses there when he came to Ireland in 1649 to put down the rebellion and massacre the Irish people. His ghost still walked the stairways and corridors.

—Must be a very busy ghost. There's nowhere he's not haunting, my father would say.

In the stone chamber where Queen Elizabeth I slept four hundred years ago, we had our classes. I liked to imagine the old queen having her feet washed by a servant, looking out this same window on a land then empty of roads and houses. Mother washed her feet sometimes by the fire, in a pink plastic basin, to ease the aches she felt after her housework.

—I had feet as white as alabaster, she reminisced.

—I had a full head of hair once, Father recalled. The finest head of wavy black hair in the whole of Ireland, all the girls loved my hair. They said I looked like Burt Lancaster.

—Mickey Mouse, you mean.

—Look at me now, anyway: an old crock, and together they laughed.

Our favorite teacher was Brother Brennigan, who taught history. History was about real people who had lived and died. Like us. It wasn't just about dates and facts.

—The English were barbarians who pillaged and destroyed wherever they went. An ignorant murderous tribe, so they were, boys, who were jealous of our glorious culture which was already thousands of years old when they were only learning to stand upright. Sure didn't they steal our land, starve us, evict and transport us. Wouldn't let us speak our language or practice our religion and told us we were apes. Our leaders and patriots were hanged or shot or driven into exile. The glorious Fenian martyrs of 1916 who sacrificed their lives for Ireland shot by a firing squad in Kilmainham Gaol after the rising of Easter Monday failed. And boys, which of you would have the courage to die for Ireland? That's what it meant to be a patriot, to die with glory for your country. So, we must learn the songs and poems about them so they will never be forgotten.

> *In Mountjoy jail*
> *One Monday morning*
> *High upon the gallows tree*
> *Kevin Barry gave his young life*
> *For the cause of liberty.*

—Flowers will grow from their blood, he told us.

There was a brother who frightened us all.

He liked to raise your fingers with the tip of his bamboo cane, then swish it through the air and beat you. His hands were hairless red lumps of things. When he leaned on a desk they were white along the knuckles. I'll never forget the calm fury of his face, the smell of stale sweat from under his cassock. I would press my fist into my eye to dull the pain of the beating, a cloud of purple ringed with gold would appear, then darkness. I bit my nails and the skin around them down to bloody stumps.

—You are a useless article. You'll be good for nothing except the pick and the shovel, the brother told me. You're a stupid bloody dunce. And what will you ever be any good for?

—I don't know, Brother.

—The pick and shovel. That's all you'll ever be any good for.

So many words he had for stupid: lump, gobdaw, dumbbell, clown, fool, dunderhead, galoot, imbecile, dolt, eejit, stumour, idiot, gooley, gobshite, donkey, dolt, clot, ass, muttonhead, amadan, gubbawn, ignoramus, ninny, ninnyhammer.

My face would furrow in fearful concentration as he growled with impatience, his viciousness awakening. Arm resting loosely over my shoulders as if we were friends, then the spitting fury, chalk screeching and breaking on the board as he would write the simple answer. He would take my hair in both hands and lift me slowly off the ground until my eyes watered.

Beyond the classroom window, I could see my hill field. I could see the ruin where the Devil played cards for the souls of gamblers, where Oisín fell from his horse and was turned into dust. I concentrated on that hill, my hands on fire for a humiliated eternity. I imagined myself out of the classroom on the open road in a caravan, like Mr. Toad from *The Wind in the Willows*, clopping along the back roads of the English countryside. Or running away with Duffy's Circus, learning how to walk the high wire with a pole, miles above the awestruck crowds. Or learning how to be a magician's assistant and get sawed in half; the thrill of knives thrown at me as I was turned on a wheel.

The brother threatened us with Letterfrack, the industrial school, a kind of prison where they sent boys who were trouble-makers. Once, in class, he hit a boy so hard that blood leaked out of his ear. He took his handkerchief and dabbed the blood dry and had him sit in the front row and said gently that a boy should be good and must not provoke him. The class ended and to make up, he let the boy lead the prayer for the grace of a happy death.

One day, something changed within us and our fear of him turned. I cannot remember whose idea it was to get him. We crouched behind a wall and waited to ambush him as he cycled out one evening for his daily jaunt to the laneways beyond the canal. The stones we threw mostly missed but for one that struck, knocking him to the ground. He lay there in a heap on the road, blood reddening his white hair, bicycle wheels still spinning. A woman helped him stand.

We fled, thrilled by our violence, over the hill like Tom Barry's guerrillas in the Civil War he was always telling us about. How they would appear from nowhere on lonely roads and ambush the British soldiers.

A few days later, he appeared before us, head and face cut, arm bandaged in a sling. All the brothers stood on top of the bicycle shed where they could be seen, like huge crows, the wind whipping around them. The head brother's voice boomed around the playground:

—I want the curs responsible for this vicious and cowardly attack to present themselves. Now.

There was silence. Nobody moved. We were all for one and one for all.

Years later, I met him walking in the street, his eyes glued to the pavement as if looking for something he'd lost. He seemed frail and stooped in an ill-fitting coat, dandruff on the collar, clumps of hair growing from his nose and ears. He had a tremor when he shook my hand. Both of us with scars; his above the eyebrow, mine invisible.

I didn't think of him again until one night, unexpectedly. I had made my London theater debut at the Royal Court Theatre in 1980. The play was a critical success, and after the performance each night we would drink in the pub next door to the theater. One night we were standing outside waiting for a cab. Behind us loitered a group of drunken soldiers, also waiting for a cab.

—Let them go first, I said to my girlfriend. If you lads want to go before us, I said, no problem. We're not in a rush.

A beefy one with a mustache focused on me.

—Are you Irish?

—Yes.

—You cunt, he said. Oi, we got an Irish cunt here. What you doing here, you fucking Irish cunt? I said what you doing in this country? Why don't you fuck off back to where you came from?

His fist smashed into my face. I went down.

They kicked my ribs, my head and face with their soldier's boots. I could hear my girlfriend shouting for the police. A man tried to stop them and he was punched.

The faces of the soldiers were frenzied. They were out of breath, screaming.

When I woke in the hospital a policeman was standing at the end of the bed. He asked me to give an account as best I could of the incident.

They had arrested the soldiers, who came from a nearby barracks. They had all returned that day from Northern Ireland. They had been on a six-month tour of duty.

—Suppose it was your accent that set them off.

The policeman asked if I wanted to press charges. He showed me their photographs. They were working-class kids, no more than eighteen or nineteen years old.

—I don't want to press charges.

I lay in the hospital bed and thought of that brother in the roadway, the wheel of his bike spinning, blood in his white hair, eyes full of bewilderment and fear.

A SATURDAY MORNING in Beverly Hills.

I woke early, a pain in my chest as if there was a broken bone in there. I held my breath and it abated, but as I breathed out it came again and I was filled with a cold fear that I was having a heart attack.

Birds sang in the trees beside the window. Was it on this ordinary day that I would die of a heart attack? In this rented house looking out to Catalina Island, still visible before the rising smog clouds?

A gardener with an engine of noise on his back blew leaves outside. I had meetings all day. Important meetings.

—No, I cannot die on a day like today, I have many years before me. I will die in bed an old man, surrounded by those I love. This is crazy thinking, I've pulled a muscle in my sleep, that's all.

Yet my breathing was ragged and the pain would not cease. Blood throbbed in the veins of my arm, and I thought that if I changed position the pain might lessen but it did not.

—Should I lie here? Two opposing voices battled; one declaring with calm reason that it would pass, the other begging me to call for help.

Down those winding canyon roads every red light was against us, my pain abating, then returning.

At the emergency room I was lowered into a wheelchair, relieved that I'd reached some kind of safe harbor. Information given, forms filled, *just a formality, sir.* I was pushed down the corridors of overhead light to a room where there were two beds. One was occupied by a man my own age who calmly observed my arrival, a friendly good-humored cove who reassured me there was nothing to worry about, that this was one of the best hospitals in California, if not in the world.

There was a relief in describing my symptoms to the doctors, and I was illogically reassured by the sports channel on the television, which showed some golfer careless of anxiety or fear in a green-grassed world. *How beautiful the world is*, I thought, *now that I'm about to leave it without the comfort of a god.*

How many have I hurt by my selfishness? Promises broken, betrayals, and lies. Do I love enough or not at all, myself above others? Am I a good father, a bad friend? Too ambitious, too quick to criticize, intolerant of the needs of others, smug? Have I been a coward, a hypocrite who can argue both sides with passionate conviction, a subtle braggart and boaster quick to take offense and slow to forgive? Entitled, proud, jealous, mean. Forgive me, I begged the universe or whoever may be up there, *forgive me for all that I've been or pretended to be. Let me just survive this and I will dedicate myself to all that is good, loving others as I love myself, honoring my place in the universe.* I became filled with a strange euphoria as I contemplated this new hopeful, generous self.

Destiny has brought you here so that your new life can begin.

I felt the doctor's cold fingers on my wrist, a stethoscope on my chest, as I searched his face for any sign of concern. Like being on a plane during turbulence. *Please just reassure me. I'm afraid.*

My mind would not settle, remembering scraps of irrelevant conversations, bits of old songs. The world would go on without me, my time here as brief as a passing cloud.

When the curtains opened, the bed beside mine was vacant. At last a nurse entered to declare brightly that she had good news for me—the doctor had looked at the tests and everything seemed normal. I'd probably just been suffering from acute indigestion, as there was absolutely nothing the matter with me.

She praised my bravery and quick thinking as wild relief rushed through me. I thanked her and could have kissed her. I thought I could love her.

Didn't I think that before, with the nurse who took care of me in the Meath Hospital when I had an emergency appendectomy years ago?

Nurse Buckley, her starched uniform stretched over the lovely apple of her behind, long hair kept from tumbling with a bun; the touch of her fingers, caring, on my forehead. Lingering by the bed to talk to me, and keeping an eye out for the battle-axe matron. Her soft Kerry accent. Antiseptic hospital smell and her forever linked in my mind.

—I'm going to have to shave you, she said.

—Ah, no thanks, I replied. Sure I don't shave yet.

And she nodded to my privates. I felt like a right stumour to not know that.

I fell in love with her because I'd never known anyone so gentle and caring.

I asked her out and took her to O'Donaghue's to show her off, but ran out of things to say because all we had in common was my appendix.

Death was vanquished, and I laughed at my fearful cowardice of the morning.

> O the bells of Hell go ting-a-ling
> For you but not for me
> O grave where is thy victory?
> Death where is thy sting?

And what of my fellow patient, bed newly made and not a sign of him ever having been there? The word the nurse used was "expired," as if he were a license or an insurance policy.

He was taking his kid to Disneyland, he was a "just to be on the safe side" admission like me.

And now his bed was empty

I was a witness to the last moments of his life. Now there was only his absence and my memory of his reassurance to me that everything would be alright.

❧

Growing up, I learned so much about acting and performance watching what my father called the theater of our street.

This is the street where my best friend, the grease monkey, lived.

I see her lean against the chip-shop wall, braless, in a tight miniskirt, radio on her shoulder, the corner boys watching her like hunters watching prey. They called her slag, said that she would ride two lads at once. She had been expelled from school for taking a hammer to one of the teachers. She gave snob girls the finger when their mouths tightened in disapproval at the sight of her. Once the parish priest gave her a lift in his new car and lectured her for wearing miniskirts and being a cause of temptation.

—The Mother of Our Lord, you can be sure, wasn't cavorting around in a miniskirt, he said.

—Yeah, and Jesus Christ didn't have a brand-new Volkswagen under his fat arse either, she retorted.

Her mother was dead and she lived with her father on the road opposite our house. He repaired broken cars for a living, his overalls blackened with grease, hair falling over his forehead as he peered into the guts of engines.

In those cars with bird shit on the windows she taught me to drive, shouting and clipping me across the head.

—I'm a grease monkey, she said, do you know what that is? It's American for car mechanic.

She showed me how to roll cigarettes and we'd sit smoking and listening to her old transistor radio.

—Dogs understand me, she said. I have a special whistle for them which makes them stop to look at me, and it was true. She loved Buddy Holly and the Everly Brothers, but Marty Robbins singing about how he fell in love with a Mexican girl in the West Texas town of El Paso was her favorite song.

She always mitched from school. The truant officer came to see her father, but really her father didn't care whether she went or not.

—The poor man, people would mutter, a widower trying to drag up a wild thing like her. But she took care of him and the house, made his fry, washed his clothes.

We would spend afternoons in the picture house, sharing cigarettes and spitting down from the balcony on the people below. Or scutting buses and trucks, stealing from the sweet-shop. We made a cart from old orange boxes, with axle and twine to steer, knocking sparks off the footpaths with ball bearing wheels, the noise frightening old people. We mixed the sticky blood of our fingers together to swear eternal loyalty and promised never to betray each other in thought, word, or deed.

Once, she squared up to a boy who insulted us.

—What you going to do about it? he taunted. You're just a stupid girl. She told him to step back and, when he didn't, she let fly a stone from her catapult. It hit him between the eyes and he stumbled away bleeding.

My friends didn't understand why I hung out with her, said I must be *bleedin' desperate*, but I wondered what it would be like to kiss her.

When I asked her if I could, she said:

—We can do more than that.

She led me across the dark of the football field to the waste ground behind the factory. It was a cold night and we found a place out of the wind. Long John Baldry's voice streamed out of her radio. She looked in my eyes and placed my hand on her breast and we kissed. But after a while she broke away.

—I can't, you're like my brother, she said.

—And you're like my sister. I can't either. And we laughed, relieved.

—Have you ever done the business with that pox bottle?

I told them I took her up behind the factory.

—Well did you ride her?

I wanted to be one of them and not have them laugh at me, so desperate to have their approval that I said yes and laughed along with them.

One of them soon told her what I'd said and how I'd bragged, and I was so ashamed to think of her face that I took the coward's way out and avoided her. She confronted me in the street, black tears of mascara running down her cheeks, her voice quiet. She told me she'd never forgive me for betraying our blood oath. We didn't speak again.

By 1973, I'd heard she was working in the shoe factory, and on my way home from university one day I saw her coming toward me, but she crossed the street to avoid me. I never saw her again after that.

Later someone told me she left Ireland, pregnant. I didn't believe them.

—The Lord knows who the father is, could be any dog or divil.

—Her own poor father drinking himself into a stupor every night since she went.

—Having to carry that cross, God love the poor man.

—But wasn't she let run like a wild animal around the place.

I never forgot her. In 2004, I was walking on a footpath among Christmas trees in Brooklyn when I heard Marty Robbins singing "El Paso," and I saw myself and the grease monkey in a convertible, speeding along the freeway to that faraway place.

They say that the songs you love when you're young will break your heart when you're old. I stood for a moment and spoke her name aloud, and asked her forgiveness, wherever she was.

⁓ꙮ⁓

This is where Ned lived, in his cottage at the crossroads. One road came from the city, another led up to the hills.

The cottage had two small windows covered with decaying lace, a door of peeling paint, a roof where rats and birds nested. No electricity.

—Here why would you not get in the electricity? Be done with all this foostering with oil and wicks and glass. Flick of the switch is all you need.

—The lamps were good enough for my father and his father before and they're good enough for me. The dawn gets us for the day just as the twilight prepares us for the night. That's the way I see it.

We'd see Ned standing outside his door. The world and his wife knew him. The walkers on their way to the hills, women pushing babies in prams, footballers heading to the pitches, coats over their shorts and jerseys, lovers heading for the secrecy of the fields; all would stop to talk with Ned about everything and nothing.

Sunday-suited in clothes from a century ago: brown cord trousers held up with an army belt and fastened at the ankles with rubber bands, striped shirt, studless and without a collar, and a wide-lapeled jacket. His old pipe burning away beneath a silver lid dotted with holes, him puffing away like a chimney.

Ned kept a few hens, sold their eggs, sometimes, or vegetables from the long garden, wrapped in newspaper, clay clinging to them still. Sometimes my mother would bring him bacon, black pudding, or curranty bread made of sugary sponge and jam.

He would sit, eating a heel of bread with jam, and read aloud the events of the world or the death notices.

—Dearly beloved husband, at his residence, funeral after ten o'clock mass. There's only two things you can be: you're either alive or you're dead, he would say, and it's better to be one than the other.

My missus, God rest her, Molly, died a long time ago. That's a photograph of her on the mantle. She used to send me to the pub to buy a naggin of whiskey for her chest. She was always at me to wrap meself up well. The east wind is a killer, she'd say. She had a great devotion to her favorite saint, the child who wore a crown and was the baby Jesus's best friend. He was called the Infant of Prague. Every night after the rosary she'd be asking the infant for this thing or that thing.

Never darkened a chapel door meself, I believe in no god, said Ned. I fought in the Irish Civil War; that's when I lost me faith, when I saw what man can do to man. When she passed on in the hospital, I held her hand till the life left her. It was the east wind got her in the end.

One day, men with briefcases arrived from the council. They wanted to give me a brand-new house. A lovely modern house, they said.

You wouldn't even have to move that far away, just a few hundred yards. Haven't you noticed that the amount of traffic from the city is increasing by the day? So much so that we have to make what we call a traffic island. I refused to move. They came again but this time I bolted the door against them. They stood on the pavement waving official papers, till finally they snapped shut their briefcases and took themselves off.

The guards arrived then, removing their caps before entering the porch, and when they came out they looked grim as a small crowd watched in silence. The priest came next. Oh, I listened respectfully but I gave him short shrift in the end when I saw what he was up to.

Then the council moved the bus stop so it is now outside me bloody bedroom window. The next thing, a fish-and-chip shop opens, then a dry cleaner's and supermarket and meself still in the cottage like a last skittle. Then they begin to build the traffic island with jackhammers and bulldozers and dumpers and, to be fair, the workers came to me and apologized, just doing a job, they have mouths to feed, and sure how could I hold it against them, I understand.

One night, a car crashed into the wall of the garden trying to avoid a lorry. The council said it was my fault because the house was in the way and that I was blocking progress as well as being a danger to life. They said I was a stubborn and selfish old man.

We will take you to jail if you don't comply, the council said, *you'll be evicted by force and that will be that.*

Take me to jail, said I. I'm not afraid. I fought to make this country free, and the men who died would be ashamed of the go-boys and bullies that are running it now, behaving like the old landlords, evicting people out of their homes.

The television cameras interviewed council members who said they fully sympathized with my position but the matter was out of their hands. The next thing, the sheriff came and dumped all me things onto the street, grandmother's clock, me books, a bed, me armchairs and wardrobe; even Dolly's crockery, with its blue willow pattern, some of it glued and cracked.

The crowd shouted: *Lackeys! Youse should be ashamed of yourselves! Evicting an old man!* I talked to Dolly that night as

I always did and she told me it was time. Next morning I came out and the crowd applauded and cheered. Without a backward glance, I walked the short distance to the new house. It's a modern thing with a tiled roof, a door, a number, and a bell, a patch of grass either side of a concrete path. I'll plant no vegetables or flowers there, and I won't allow the priest to come and bless it.

In Ned's new house, at night, behind the venetian blinds, the oil lamps burned.

~༄༅~

This is the street where Jimmy Mulligan used to live.

He played for the school football team and we all thought he was a brilliant goalkeeper who one day would play for Manchester United. I will never forget that day soon after we were set free from school and we fled, wild and joyous, into the eternal days of summer.

We collected stamps, marbles, and chestnuts, swam, made masks out of cornflake packets, swapped comics, played football, thought about girls. The lush boredom of Sunday afternoons—car doors open, men with handkerchiefs on their heads listening to football—would have us headed for the river. Three of us: me, Jimmy, and a lad whose father was a soldier and had gone to Africa to serve with the United Nations. We never stopped talking.

—What would you do if you met a bear?

—There's no bears in Ireland.

—Yeah but say, if you met one.

—I'd give him a root in the bollocks.

—My da knows a man who was attacked by a rat.

—People had to eat rats in the siege of Derry.

—A snake bit a boy in the mickey. Came up out a toilet. It was in the paper.

—A snake could swallow a whole cow.

—We saw Oliver Plunkett's head.

—Who's he?

—The English hung, drawn, and quartered him for being holy.

—Dr. Crippen killed all those women and everyone thought he was a nice man.

—Like Mr. Rogers. He looks like a killer.

—I can make myself sneeze by looking at the sun.

—Show us then.

—If there was sun I would.

—I can make a fire with a magnifying glass.

—If you go to the back of the fence in the sports ground, you can see into the women's changing rooms.

—No, you can't.

—Do trains turn around in stations?

—You're mental. They don't turn around.

—Well how do they get to face the other way?

—Do nuns go to the toilet?

—You can get the pox off a toilet seat.

—I can talk like an American.

—There was a boy who died from being struck from lightning. Went in through his ears. It'll go in any hole you have.

—In your arsehole even?

Our favorite place was the roaring river where we could jump whooping from the bridge, knees to chest, crashing into the silent underworld to touch the stones on the bottom. Jimmy was always the best at holding his breath. Last to burst the water with a screech of triumph, louder than the thunder of the falling ford water, and in between, we wrestled and chased each other and dozed on the banks in the sun. We never heard him cry for help. He must have.

A man saw his hand reach out of the water and disappear again and shouted:

—That kid is in trouble!

What I remember is his screaming over and over:

—He's drowning. He's drowning.

And he dived in, and there was screaming and shouting and calling his name, and we dived again and crashed and flailed to where we thought he was.

He was messing with us surely, but it wasn't funny. He would appear laughing and we would give him a bollocking. We kept going down, stayed till they thought our lungs would burst, but there was nothing but weeds and green tendrils we called giant's hair swirling in the dark water. The afternoon went quiet and there were crowds of people looking from the bridge, and the traffic backed all the way to the town. A man fishing for pinkeens with his kids found Jimmy twisted in brambles a few hundred yards away where the current had carried him, and they pulled him out and laid him on the riverbank.

And I still wanted to say, Come on, Jimmy, stop acting the bollocks.

We were weeping great, choking sobs.

—Out of his depth, he must have been, a woman was saying. God help his mother and father getting this news.

I remember thinking that maybe I was asleep, in a dream, and my mother would wake me up for school. The guards were on the bridge waving people on. We could hear the ambulance siren in the distance. Jimmy was lying wrapped in a woman's red coat.

So slight he was underneath it, his hair plastered over his forehead, eyes closed as if he were asleep and nothing was the matter at all.

The ambulance came and a path was cleared. A guard told everyone to stand back, and the slow way they moved, and their faces, told the story that there was no hope. The traffic was backed all the way up to the village; people stood outside their cars, hands over their mouths, drawing children to them, watching in silence as the ambulance doors closed.

His face wasn't scary like Mrs. Gordon dressed in a black gown, a little picture of her husband beside her. She looked like someone else without her glasses, which always made her eye so big. The good eye was closed and the bad one staring at the wall.

Life is gone away out of him, that's what it means to be dead, I thought.

Candles flickered on either side of Jimmy's bed as if someone was breathing gently on the flames, making shadows on the walls. The room was crowded and the grown-ups knelt to mumble the rosary. There was a smell of wet wool and sweat and burning wax.

Later when it had stopped raining, I went out to see if any stars were falling because that was a sure sign a person was in Heaven. I waited and watched for a long time but no star fell. I remembered Mrs. Gordon telling me how all the constellations had their own stories of how they came to be, that the sky was full of chariots and animal warriors and gods from the time at the beginning of the world.

The moon was like a ghost boat floating in the night.

—He was a champion goalkeeper, said Jimmy's father. He could have played for Ireland. I often said that to him, so he could have.

I started to feel the back of my throat closing over, so I ran out until I came to the hill we used to gallop down, pretending to be cowboys and Indians, hoping that Jimmy might somehow see me when I galloped on my pretend lone horse in the moonlight. Down the dusty Wild West hill, remembering when we were gunslingers together and didn't know that God would call Jimmy away, as the priest said. But the strangest thing was that I couldn't remember Jimmy's face. I could only find an image of him climbing up the air, his hand reaching out; not drowning, but making another glorious save for Manchester United.

~~~⦿⧉⦿~~~

This is where Paganini the plumber lived. Every evening, in thick boots, overalls shinning with oil, he would thump down our street. His wife, a bony woman from the country, sprinkled him with holy water before he entered the house, then closed the door on nosey parkers.

I was friends with their son and used to eat with them if both my parents were at work. His wife always had his dinner ready for him, spiked his potatoes with a fork to test that they were done just so, cut his meat into squares, poured a pint of water from the tap, and then sat opposite as he recounted his day's adventures from the world of plumbing.

Paganini lent me records, which he held by the edges, carefully, with his oil-blackened fingers. Mahler and Dvořák and Bruckner. I pretended to listen to them, as I didn't want to disappoint him, but we didn't have a record player and if we had, I would have been listening to Pink Floyd. I thought Paganini's taste in music was out-of-date and irrelevant.

After dinner, he'd go to the sitting room to smoke and listen to the news. Then he'd take out his violin and play standing by the window. When he played, he seemed to go to some secret place, like the actors and singers I'd seen in the theater. When he finished playing, he'd place the violin back in its velvet-lined case as tenderly as putting a baby into a crib to sleep.

When Paganini suffered from what people called "his nerves," you wouldn't hear the violin for weeks. Or months. Once we didn't hear it for nearly a year. His walk would lose its energy, he'd stop saying hello to people, and he'd take to bed. Then one day he'd saunter down the street, whistling, and we would hear his violin again through the window.

Paganini's ghost was there when I attended the Cannes Film Festival in 1995 for the premiere of *The Usual Suspects*. As we walked up those red-carpeted steps, hundreds of photographers shouted, the clicks of their flashes sounding as if we were being shot at. The audience gave the film a ten-minute standing ovation and we also stood to acknowledge the applause.

—You are in a fucking hit, dude, someone said.

At the after-party there were crowds of handshaking, hugging strangers and beautiful women. Dawn came up over the Croisette. I staggered back to my room with a pocketful of phone numbers, ignoring the feeling of dislocation rising in me, the sense of being physically there but somewhere else in my head. I stood on the balcony of the hotel, looking out at the beautiful day breaking on the Riviera. I knew I wouldn't sleep now.

—You know this changes everything, a famous producer had said at the party, bear-hugging me and whispering in my ear, You're a fucking star.

I had recoiled, embarrassed at the word.

Billionaires' yachts bobbed on the water in the dawn light. I ran in the empty streets, hoping to give the slip to the darkness spreading like a stain inside my brain. I ran and ran, past fluttering flags, the billboards for a thousand movies, running up into the hills of gated villas, hidden by bougainvillea and cypress trees. But when I stopped, there was still such tumult in my mind I was afraid I would fall down and be found weeping in the street.

I returned to the hotel, sweating, the foyer already filled with journalists and publicists and television cameras ready for the next twenty-five films to be shown that day. There was a poster featuring our film, a review printed large and a photograph of us all with the heading "Best film of the festival." A triumph.

Black coffee was put in my hand and I was politely bossed from interview to interview. When we emerged into the sunlight for lunch, the paparazzi were there again, calling all our names. We now needed bodyguards. Toasts were drunk, more phone numbers exchanged. A girl said, smiling:

—I need your key to turn me on.

Voices began to echo and I felt myself disappearing, as if underwater, gulping for breath.

I was taken by car to a photo shoot. I remember a wall and the sea glinting and the photographer ordering me to look this way, chin up, look that way. Now down. How about a smile?

—Just take the bloody photograph.

I must have packed. Made some excuse, though I don't recall what. I remember the hot wind coming through the car window as we sped along the motorway toward Nice.

I must have checked into the hotel, shown my passport and credit card, but the next thing I recall I was in bed. It was the afternoon, the curtains were closed. I could not leave the room, or the bed. I was behind enemy lines, free-falling in a soundless hole, the thin light above disappearing.

To a God I no longer believed in, I prayed:

—Have pity on my lostness. Don't let my days bleed into each other like this. I am unraveling inside. Can you not see the terror that consumes me? I was without even a spark of hope. I had been exhausted by the act of living, worn out by the smallest task.

Why did I feel so worthless, of no merit, superfluous to the world?

All I wanted was to be left alone in this dark room. I was afraid that if something cracked inside me, I might become insane. Where yesterday the world had had such meaning, today it had none. It seemed that overnight, my world had completely changed. The transformation was overwhelming. I had no desire to eat, stared in a stupor at the television. I felt unable to care about anything. The first dark thought gave birth to another and then another and became reality. I sought refuge only in sleep but even then I couldn't escape. I dreamt I was standing on the banks of a frozen lake and someone was telling me not to cross it. I woke struggling for breath.

Nobody knew where I was. In that room in a French hotel I remembered Paganini and how he would disappear too. And like him I awoke one morning several days later and the black dog had left. I opened the curtains, the light poured in like a blessing, and I emerged weak and tentative, ashamed of fleeing a moment of huge success; ashamed, but determined again to join the world.

I CAN'T HELP but imagine how different my life could have been had I remained on my once chosen path to the priesthood. In 1961, a new curate visited our school and announced to the class:

—Boys, I want to talk to you about vocations to the priesthood. A vocation is a word from Latin meaning "to call." God might be calling you, he said. And if he is, you must answer.

I thought of God trying to get through to me on the phone. The curate continued:

—If you listen to the voice deep inside yourself, in quiet moments, you will hear him. To be chosen is the greatest gift any family could have.

The curate showed us slides of missionaries in straw hats, flying planes, crossing rivers and jungles in faraway countries like Bolivia, living a life of adventure like they were in *The Hotspur* comic. He passed photographs around the class: smiling men surrounded by laughing children. He stood under a map of the world, pointing to places I had never heard of: Papua New Guinea, Tobago, Liberia.

And sure enough, I began to hear God. It started as a feeling. And it became more and more real and insistent. When I was praying in the empty chapel one day, I became convinced that I had a vocation, and it filled me with great joy. I had seen the booklets in the church porch of young lads with dodgy haircuts, beatific smiles gazing heavenward to answer the call to the priesthood. *Follow me*, they said under a picture of Jesus with a beard.

The curate gave me a magazine with an article about a seminary in England which received boys my age who wished to train for the priesthood. There were photographs of them playing snooker and football and of older boys studying in their own rooms, surrounded by shelves of books as sunlight streamed in through the windows.

My own room. In our house I shared a bed with my two brothers, my three sisters slept together in another room across the hallway.

—Put up your hands, the boys who would like to follow the Lord. To save the souls of heathens.

I saw myself, in that moment, on a horse, in a straw hat, a snow-capped blue mountain behind, crossing rivers full of crocodiles, hacking my way through jungle. I raised my hand.

—I've decided I want to become a priest.

—What? said a friend. Are you mad or what? You're going to be a monk?

—A priest.

—Same difference.

—You're only eleven! You have to be old to be a priest!

—It takes a long time to study.

—How long?

—Twelve years. That's why I have to go to a seminary. To learn how to say mass and give communion and hear people's confessions.

—Bless me Father, for I have sinned. I was pulling me flute.

—Then, I have to go out to Papua New Guinea.

—For what?

—To convert heathens.

—Where do you have to go?

—A gaff in England. I can't pronounce its name. Near Birmingham.

—They have a crap football team. Just got relegated to the second division.

I was beginning to get cold feet. Then a clothing list arrived.

Grey flannel trousers—2
Black shoes—2
Shirts—5
Socks & underwear—7
Blazer—1
Cap—1
Sports rig-out
Toiletries

It was too late. I was too afraid to say I had changed my mind. I had to go through with it.

I left for the seminary one night in October. The streetlights pulsed weakly against a thickening fog. Neighbors and family came to the house to give a little party for my departure. They pressed coins and notes into my hand, Miraculous Medals to keep me safe for the journey on the night mailboat across the Irish Sea.

—O Lord, save us! He's only a traneen to be going to England, my aunt sniffled.

My father had promised to be home before I left, but when it came time there was no sign of him. I heard my mother whisper that he couldn't face saying goodbye, and he'd be in the pub waiting until we were well gone. Now I wanted nothing more than to stay, not leave for another country, at eleven years old, to become a priest. Until that moment, I had not realized how much I was going to miss my home.

I thought of my father teaching me to ride a bicycle, how he held onto the saddle as I wobbled the handlebars. How by the fire in the early morning we would listen to the radio, to the fights from Madison Square Garden; the strange nasal accent of the commentator in the crackling static, the names Rocky Marciano, Sonny Liston, Floyd Patterson, Jack Dempsey, the Manassa Mauler. Or how he would wake me at dawn to go out in the still-asleep world beyond the town to pluck mushrooms from dewed grass. We'd fill the bucket, then go home to a feast, sizzling in the butter of the pan.

—We better be off or this fog will be down on us, said Mr. Lyons, the neighbor who would drive my mother and me to the boat.

—Is there any sign of him?

—Perhaps he won't be able to leave if the fog comes down too thickly.

Then my father came like a ghost out of the fog, swaying slightly. He shook my hand, told me to write to my mother because she'd be worrying. I could tell he'd had a few drinks, his voice trying to be light and cheerful.

—Your tea is on the table, my mother said, annoyed, and he went into the house. My mother got into the car and it gave a small sigh with her weight. I climbed in beside her.

—Have you got everything? she asked me.

And then I remembered my comics and ran back inside the house. Behind the kitchen door, I heard my father weeping.

On the road to the boat, the fog felt like a wall I passed through, as if from my old self to a newer one, and just beyond the golf club, having blindly inched our way, it cleared. Lights lined the coast from Howth all the way to Wexford. Gulls screamed in the wind.

The mailboat left the land—though it felt like the land was leaving us, drawing back into the darkness, churning up a path of foam behind it. A fierce wind knifed along the deck. A nun vomited politely into a paper bag; her sisters stood protectively around her, their veils swirling madly about them. A man held to the rails, a parcel against his chest as though he were a child hugging a pillow. All these people emigrants and me now one of them.

My uncle left his family's small farm for Texas when I was a child. He remained in that faraway place for forty years, always sick for Ireland until he returned from the warm sun to the wet fields and grey stone walls of his boyhood. The village so quiet a dog crossing the street was an event, and on winter afternoons when the sky turned dark early he began to long once more for warmth and light, and he became an exile again, leaving this time for good.

My mother often recalled the night before he left. Their little house crowded with neighbors, music, dancing, and drinking. But such sadness underneath all the gaiety. Now she was watching me leave with a suitcase for the first time in my short life.

I could hear live music coming from the bar below deck. Hornpipe on a concertina. My father played the button accordion. The folds had flames painted on them and when he pushed them together it sounded like a person sighing or like a small animal's cry.

—The notes are alive, he would say, but you have to coax them out of their hiding places because they are shy like a person can be, and will only come out for people who love them.

He wanted me to learn and become a better player than he because he played by ear, bits and scraps he knew from growing up. He wanted me to be able to read the notes so I could play any piece of music.

My parents sent me to study at the home of Mr. King, each lesson costing one shilling. My mother and I arrived at a house with a wild garden and were shown by a sulky-faced girl into a room, bare except for a piano with a metronome ticking loudly on top. A feeble flame sputtered in the grate, and when a downward breath of wind blew smoke into the room, the girl cursed it for a devil. We sat and waited until at last Mr. King himself entered.

He wore a cravat and a torn cardigan and his hair was silver and long down his back. He reminded me of a lion.

—Play something for me till I see. He held a bamboo cane and touched my fingers with it to steer me away from wrong notes. I started attending lessons once a week. He taught me slow Irish airs, and, later, little waltzes, tarantellas, and such things. The first song I learned properly by reading was "The Whistling Gypsy." He sang along with me.

> *The whistling gypsy came over the hill*
> *Down through the valley so shady*
> *He whistled and he sang*
> *Till the green woods rang*
> *And he won the heart of a lady.*

He told me about the tunes and the stories behind them.

—Facts are in books; if you want to know what people feel, it's in music. All the feelings and all the music of the world can be put down in seven notes: do, re, mi, fa, sol, la, ti.

He had great reverence for the songs of leaving and yearning.

I was drawn down below by the music. Men leaned against the counter, talking loudly, laughing, drinking pints as if they were not at sea at all. A couple of musicians played, eyes closed, feet beating time on the floor. Someone shouted a yahoo of encouragement. Some of the accents were English and others a mix of English and Irish, but most were Irish, from the country.

There were ten other boys like me dressed in black, belted coats and caps with a white badge, an eagle rising over Latin words. All of us in short trousers. I bought a plate of chips, poured vinegar and ketchup over them, and sucked orange juice through a straw for the first time. The label was an English one I'd never seen before.

One of the boys challenged me:

—I bet you wouldn't swallow a bottle of vinegar. My face flamed. How much would you give me if I did?

—I'd give you a shilling.

I pulled the top off the bottle, put it to my mouth, and drank until it was empty. The sour burn teared at my throat and chest. The other boys looked at me in silence.

I took the money. My insides were a roaring fire but I made it to the deck before my vomit got sucked away by the wind into the darkness. I slid down behind the slatted seats and fell asleep. When I woke, the lights of Wales appeared.

The passengers lined up to disembark, shunting along with their cases, carrying sleeping children. The boat moved sideways to the dock, men waiting for the ropes to be thrown to them to secure around the bollards. With a shudder, the engines went silent. It was two thirty in the morning. I'd never stayed awake that late in my life. The clouds had moved and the stars were showing. The night air smelled sea-salty. I thought how the Welsh moon was in the same sky as in Ireland, and that gave me a warm feeling.

As we walked toward the custom hall, a policeman in a pointed helmet with the Queen's emblem on it watched impassively. The customs men went through the folded clothes of the woman in front. Brown cases, some tied with belts, were hoisted onto the table and clicked open for inspection. We tried to make small talk with the unsmiling officers rooting through our clothes.

I felt a sense of pride when I displayed the folded shirts my mother had packed for me. It meant I came from a neat and tidy house, and the customs man would know that and be impressed. But he didn't look up, just pushed my case along the counter. A belt of sadness hit me.

The Birmingham train was red, not the green of home. The wet smoke of the engine engulfed my face. People were already seated. A pale child in its mother's arms looked at us through the clouded glass. My mouth was sour and dry, bile still forcing its way up my throat from the vinegar.

—The worst winter in fifty years, I heard someone say.

At last, the flag was raised, and the whistle blew. The train pulled into the night past empty, lighted platforms and high black hills. The clackety-clickety-clickety-clack rhythm of steel on track seemed to beat out what my heart was repeating: *I want to go home.*

The towns, fields, hedges, roadways of Wales and then England sped by so fast I couldn't read their names. Lights of houses, here and there.

We wondered what this place we were traveling to would be like. Would it be like the Christian Brothers? Would they have canes and leathers and chair legs to hit you? New Street station in Birmingham was huge: vaulted, grimy glass. We poured into the café for hot milky tea, fried eggs, and bread. The stationmaster leaned against the counter, hat on the table to show he was off duty. We counted out our coins.

—No darlings, not Irish money. No good here. You're in England now.

The grey-dawn, grimy streets of Birmingham, then the snow-sheeted countryside of black-timbered houses, till at last we came to a village, Dickensian names on the shop fronts: Crump Undertakers; Turnbull Sweet Shop; the Barley Mow Inn; Bullocks Café.

When we finally reached the seminary, its gates opened to reveal a frozen lake. I recognized it from the photographs the curate had passed around that day in school. We plodded, one after the other, toward a house of peeling yellow paint.

The knocker echoed deeply.

A priest appeared. He was wearing Chelsea boots beneath his cassock.

—Ah. The Irish brigade.

We entered the seminary's dark, statued corridors, climbed its stairways of uneven worn stone. Paintings of dead priests and the smell of boiled cabbage hung in every room. The dormitories contained rows of narrow beds, with each of our numbers on the frame and lockers for our clothes beside them.

In the refectory the priests sat on a dais. Nuns served food from cauldrons pushed on trolleys. A priest rang a small bell for silence. We Irish boys had to stand and introduce ourselves. Whistles and clapping, and some of them laughed at our Irish accents.

❧

I was a seminarian now, on the road to priesthood and a life of prayer, study, and discipline. Yet the real world was always close by.

My body was starting to change, and my legs were in pain because they were stretching, but still I was afraid I would always be small, like Mouse Malone, our neighbor.

—You could slip him under a door if you forgot your key, as my mother would say.

My mind was full of imaginings that I kept to myself.

I used to look at myself in the mirror and fear that I was growing breasts. On the football field, whenever I was cold or I ran, my nipples felt like lumps in my shirt, so I used sticking plaster to push them down. I thought the other fellows were laughing at me, so I hunched my shoulders when I walked. Other times I would stick out my chest—but that would make them seem more pronounced. I was afraid they were going to keep growing and growing until I would have to wear a brassiere. I'd heard there were people like that, who were neither one thing nor the other, neither a boy nor a girl.

One day, I saw an advertisement in a bodybuilder's magazine. A man called Charles Atlas, who had huge muscles, promised a body like his in eight weeks. I sent off for the special offer.

I received elastic bands and a book of exercises. I hid them under the bed and took them out when everyone in the dorm was asleep, and did the stretches and pulls in my vest because I was ashamed to look at my own chest. One night the elastic snapped and the handle hit me in the eye. It turned black and bloodshot and I had to make up a lie about banging into a door.

I could not stop looking at other boys' bodies, to see how they compared with mine. I envied the ones with straight backs and wide shoulders—or those with hair on their legs, the stubbled beginnings of beards and the rasp when they rubbed their chins. I felt ashamed of my hairless, humped, big-breasted body, my broken hooter of a nose. A fellow had joked one day that my nose could scrape mice out of a hole.

I would beg the mirror to reflect another version of me; handsome and hairy and normal. I'd seen fellows in the dressing room, their flutes swinging between their legs. They looked different to my own—all sizes and shapes.

Is the skin which grows over the tip normal? I was afraid to ask anyone, and ashamed—should a boy studying to be a priest be thinking of such things?

One of the fellows told me if I caught a thing called syphilis, I would die, blind, in agony, in a madhouse.

—You get it from tugging at yourself, he said. Syphilis. That would be how I would go. The reward I would get for abusing myself to photographs in nudist health magazines with naked women throwing beach balls to each other.

Then it was gonorrhea, which you could get from toilet seats and there was no cure for. You would know you had it if you had scabs on your mouth and your piss was yellow.

One day I broke down and confessed to a boy from Newcastle that I was afraid I was going to die from syphilis and gonorrhea.

—Have you been with brassers?

—What's a brasser?

—A prozzie.

—A Protestant?

—Crikey, you don't know nothing, Paddy. A prostitute. 'Cause that's the only way you can get the clap.

I felt like new life had been given to me and I said a secret prayer.

—I promise I'll never ever be at myself ever again.

Yet even as I swore it, I was thinking of a photograph from *Life* magazine with all the girls lying out bronzed by the swimming pool in bikinis, folded neatly under the mattress, waiting.

The priest who taught us was kind and encouraged me. I wanted to be the best student he ever had; he was the most beloved teacher in the seminary. We all wanted to be his friend. His voice was gentle, and he listened to us with understanding and compassion. One of my classmates said one day:

—You're his favorite. That's why he has you sit in the front row, so that he can be near his pet.

One evening, when I returned to study hall from dinner, I was told to go to the priest's room, in the old part of the house. The students were rarely allowed up there; only the nuns had permission so they could clean or make the beds.

Up the unfamiliar staircase I climbed—nervous, maybe I'd done something for which I would be reprimanded. In the hallway, there was an odor of cigarette smoke, and I could hear piano music coming from inside the room. The priest opened the door in a red dressing gown.

That is a strange thing, I thought, *for a priest to be dressed like that.*

Inside the room, a fire burned. The window overlooked the yard of the old stables. The chairs were of worn leather and the shelves were full of books, against which leaned a few photographs I took to be of his parents. I had never been in a room like that, so cozy and welcoming, unlike the cheerless dormitories we slept in. The priest bade me sit on the sofa beside him. He smelled of aftershave; the record turned on the player.

—What kind of music do you like? he asked.

At home I used to lie under the covers listening to the BBC—late-night jazz, Bill Evans, Oscar Peterson, Stan Getz. The music took me away to New York or Paris, to lonely windswept streets and smoky clubs where hipsters in dark glasses and polo-necks lounged, listening to the breathy sax of Coleman Hawkins or to Buddy Rich's brushes on the snare, soft like falling rain. And the silence once the music ended would remind me of the echo of the mass bell dying away.

—I love Chopin, said the priest. He was from Poland, but he died, exiled, in Paris. Did you know that? All his music is about longing. When he died, his friends brought earth from his native place and threw it over his coffin. He was an exile—like you, he said in his soft voice, like satin.

He asked if I missed home.

—Yes, I said, my father and mother and sometimes my friends.

—I'm sure there must a girl who misses you too.

I thought of the girl who sang in the choir, who sat beside me all the way to Portmarnock the day the altar boys went to the seaside; and how we sang together on the train coming back, my face reddened by sun, and sand in my shoes; we stood in the swaying corridor and our bodies touched and she didn't pull away, and I thought that meant she loved me. Whenever I heard the song we sang on the train, I would think of her face and it seemed the song was about her. But I didn't want to tell the priest this, because he would think it wasn't what a boy studying to be a priest should be thinking.

The priest took a cigarette from a silver case and offered me one.

—It's alright. It'll be our secret. He winked.

I wondered: *How does the priest know this?* Had someone snitched, or had he seen me in smokers' corner, laughing and smoking among the tombstones in the graveyard?

He closed the case again with a snap. The fire flamed in the grate as the coals collapsed in the silence. It was so hot in the room, and I was beginning to sweat. I avoided looking at the priest's leg, white and hairy, when he stood to change the record.

—And do you think about girls? It's not a sin if you do. It's natural. You see, the female is put on the earth to be the spiritual and sexual companion of man in marriage. And couples enjoy the pleasure of each other's bodies. But we have taken a vow of celibacy which means we forego the physical pleasures of the body. Tell me: Do you know what procreation is?

It was a word I had never heard before. My tongue felt like a worm in my mouth because I didn't want to answer and disappoint him. The priest then told me it came from Latin.

—When a man and a woman lie together, it means they make love. Our Blessed Lord bestows on them the gift of sexual pleasure for the purpose of bringing babies into the world.

Making love: you know what that is? I'm sure you've heard the other boys talk about it, and maybe they have other ways of saying it. Maybe they laugh and joke about it. Or tell you it's something dirty. That's how we all came to be here on earth. Every single person in the world is the product of sexual desire. Your father and mother made love and you were born, and they did that through the pleasure of sex.

When people do this, they touch each other, and they become excited in a sexual way. The husband's penis becomes hard and he enters his wife's vagina, which is the opening between her legs, and he ejaculates his semen. That is how a baby is made.

I looked at the priest, but I did not know what to say. I felt like my face was aflame.

—Of course, your penis can become hard outside the sacrament of marriage, like when you have certain thoughts. Have you ever had any thoughts that make your penis hard?

I was ashamed to think the priest knew this.

—Maybe when you think about a girl you like? Or even a boy? You must have a friend and when you think about him in a certain way, it makes you want to touch yourself. Tell me: have you ever kissed a girl?

When I was younger, if actors kissed in the films, I didn't like it and would boo and shout *Skip! Skip!* at the screen along with the other kids. But lately I had been thinking about kissing and practiced on my fingers like the film actors. How desperately I'd wanted to kiss the choir girl on her mouth that day coming back from the sea after the heat of the sun and having watched her running from the waves, her long pale legs, her tight black swimsuit covering her secret body. I'd heard fellows brag about girls they knew who kissed with tongues in dark cinemas. My lust was relentless.

The priest said he liked that I was a shy boy and that I was his favorite pupil and that is why he liked to have me near, in the front seat.

Did he know about the magazine I had hidden behind the cistern in the toilets, with the pictures of girls with no clothes on playing volleyball? That made me touch myself over and over again, sinning as if the Devil himself was making me do it? When it was happening, I cared about nothing until it ended in shuddering ecstasy. And always I was consumed with shame, until the next time when I was powerless to resist.

The priest poured wine into my glass. The sofa creaked as he sat closer.

I remembered a day in summer in the countryside on my holidays.

—Why don't you bring the men their bit of grub in the field? my aunt said.

They were cutting the hay, and the men had said that I could help the stompers atop the hayrick, as I wasn't strong enough to be a forker. She placed the tea and milk bottles into the basket filled with butter and fresh currant bread, some cheese and ham, a bit of relish to sweeten it, and a Swiss roll for afters. I walked over the road and through the little grove, careful not to spill a drop. When they saw me, the men stopped their work and wiped their foreheads.

—Here comes himself with the grub.

—What have we in here be the hokey man, they said, rooting in the basket. They sat down on a blanket with their backs to the ricks of hay. A big lad from the town handed me a cigarette.

—Take a drag out of that and mind it doesn't go to your head. I pushed the smoke out through my nose. It felt good to be a man like them.

After they had eaten, one of the lads said:

—Why don't you get into the blanket and we'll give you a bit of an old see-saw Margery Daw before you go?

I got in and they made a boat and swung me over and back; then they went higher and higher till I felt I was going up to the clouds. I began to feel afraid, like the day in the swinging boats in the carnival. Their voices suddenly sounded very far away, and I started to cry in the blanket until at last they let me down.

—Sure it was only for a bit of an old laugh, they said.

Then one of them put his hands between my legs. Some of the others did too, and they started to tickle me till I was crying and laughing and excited and afraid.

When I arrived home, my aunt was angry.

—Where's the lunch things and my good cups and the empty bottles? she said.

I didn't want to tell her what the lads in the field had done for fun. I didn't know why I had run away as fast as I could and left all the lunch things and them laughing behind me, because of my being such a big crybaby, and I felt ashamed for spoiling their fun.

The priest's breath was sour and hot as he moved toward me. Then there was blackness.

Even years later it feels like the night has been concreted over. I've been picking at it with a pin ever since, afraid to use a jack-hammer, afraid of what's buried in there. I looked up a photograph of him on the internet; he was with missionaries, somewhere tropical. He smiled at the camera, his arms around two boys. They were smiling too. He had no priest's collar on, just a blue, open-necked denim shirt. His hair was long and grey. He didn't look like himself at all.

For so long I blamed myself. Ashamed and guilty that I had done something wrong. There was a tear in the side of my trousers from where I'd been roughhousing in the gym. When he put his hand into the tear I was mortified that he'd know I was wearing football shorts instead of underwear.

It was because I was so good in class studying so hard to please him, wasn't it? I wanted the praise of his gentle voice. I thought this as I lay in bed after what happened, wide awake in the sleeping dormitory. I was baffled. Yes, baffled, that was the feeling, yet it was him, so it must have been alright. Mostly I was relieved when he didn't say anything about my football shorts beneath my torn trousers.

I met an old couple in Queens, New York. She had survived the death camps with her mother. I asked her if she forgave the Germans and she replied that she had to, otherwise they'd have won. Her husband banged the table so hard the crockery jumped and we were all startled.

—There is no such thing, he shouted, as forgiveness. His eyes were hard and angry.

The day I visited Dachau I thought of them as I watched the carefree children playing on the grass. There were butterflies in the wildflowers.

I thought about the boy we knew from a few streets over who was sent away by the court to Letterfrack in the wilds of Connemara because he stole a bicycle from outside the bookies.

I remembered the boy's sad-eyed, pinched face; his torn jersey, fingers stained deep brown with nicotine. He hadn't been going to school anymore, but he'd hang around the sweetshop, smoking.

—It is a gaff way away out in the country, miles from anywhere, just bogs and rain and the Connemara wind, he'd told us. They make us work, stitching clothes and digging potatoes in the fields even in the winter. The fuckin' priests and brothers? They did things to lads. In the showers and in their beds or out in the fields.

—Like what things? we'd asked him.

—Like what things? we'd said again when he was silent.

—They'd make you suck on their mickeys. They'd put Vaseline on your arsehole and put their things in your arse, even when you cried because of the pain, and they beat you black and blue till you stopped.

I had looked wide-eyed at the boy back then, unable to comprehend what he was saying.

❧ ⁓⁓ ❧

In 2002, standing in my living room in New York, I lifted the phone and asked for the priest.

—Who may I say is calling?

—An old pupil of his.

—Let me see if he is available. He might be sleeping.

The clunk of the phone being put down. Heels across a floor. The sound of a door opening, swinging back again. Silence. Then footsteps across the floor, the phone lifted.

—Hello? he said, as if asking a question.

My mouth was dry. A hard swallow.

—You probably don't remember me. You used to teach me.

—Oh. His voice: smooth as satin still, and curious.

I told him the year. The class number.

—Mm, he said, that's a long time ago. My memory isn't what it used to be, I regret to say.

—I used to sit in the front row. I was from Dublin. I was very good at Latin. You said I was the best student you ever had.

—Oh. And what is your name again?

—You don't remember me?

—No, he said. I felt him smile politely, I'm sorry—

—I've never forgotten you. Ever.

His voice. As warm, as charming and seductive as it had been all those years ago, as if no time had passed.

—Well, that is nice when a student calls to say a nice thing.

I couldn't think of anything else to say. My anger faltered and stumbled. There was another silence.

—Are you still there? he asked.

—I'm still here.

—It was nice to talk with you. I must go. The bell is ringing for benediction. I mustn't be late. It is so kind of you to call.

I wanted in those last seconds to call him a cunt and say that even though I don't believe in Hell, I hope he does, because I want him to be terrified and burn forever.

But I said nothing. Some part of me did not want to hurt an old man with a kindly voice stuck in a retirement home who now had no memory of me or of anything he'd done.

❧

Once, at the seminary, the boy we called the Owl pissed himself in the chapel during mass because he knew we were coming for him. It wasn't enough to call him names anymore, or give him a "French bed" with ketchup in the sheets, or flatten him in the mud on the soccer field, or tear up letters he received from his people, or, as we did just one time, draw a Hitler mustache on a photograph of his mother.

His country way of talking was laughed at. We imitated his peculiar loping walk, his too-tight pants, his dark hair that fell in a fringe over the palest face, his scared eyes huge behind his ill-fitting spectacles. That's why he was called the Owl.

He was in the Christmas pantomime. He was jeered at, but he sang on, finding courage in some place inside himself until everyone went quiet. He was called a swot, though he was no more diligent about his studies than others. In his refusal to be cowed, he attained a dignity which further enraged those who despised him.

After science, we had a free period when students could walk in the grounds, play music, or read. When we came for him, he was beneath the cedar tree reading. The book cover read, *The Canterbury Tales.* When he looked up, he would have seen a crowd of maybe twenty boys closing in on him. Someone tore his book from him and threw it at him.

—The fucking Canterbury Tales. That's a nancy's book, I'll bet.

The Owl ran through the bushes, which cut his face, and out into the soccer field, where he was overtaken after he tripped and fell. Someone took his glasses off and smashed them underfoot.

—Hey four-eyes, they called. Then they took his shoes and threw them over the hedge. He kicked out blindly, his legs were grabbed, and he fell to the ground. They tore his pants off and then laughed at his colored underpants.

—What's the matter? Your people can't afford to get you proper girls' knickers?

One of the small boys from my form reached in and punched the Owl's head, then looked around for approval.

—Let's duck him in the lake! someone shouted. It was a winter's day and the water was covered with a thin ice.

They pulled off the rest of his clothes. He stood, his white body shivering. He was whacked across the backside with a stick.

—Down, beast. Grovel to your betters, said the fellow who pushed the Owl to his knees, and beg. The Owl did not reply.

—I said kneel, fairy boy, before your betters and beg.

Still he did not reply. A senior boy crushed his neck with a foot.

—Your last chance, peasant.

Still no response from the shivering body, protecting his privates with his hands.

—Look at his little todger! It's all shriveled, they laughed.

But the Owl was not afraid as he'd been in the chapel or when he was running. Something had broken in him, or had strengthened in him—it was hard to tell.

They lifted him again by the legs and arms and ran with him to the water's edge and counted to three, and then for an eternity of moments he was in the air before he hit the ice, which splintered and made a sound like wood snapping, and the Owl clawed frantically at the air. A great cheer went up. He disappeared under the water.

Then there was silence. The fellows looked from one to the other. Worry in their faces. Suddenly the Owl burst through the surface, gasping for breath. He was spluttering and swallowing water and there was silence as he sank below again through the broken ice in the green-black water.

Panicked looks between the fellows, and then he broke the surface again, vomiting. Someone reached a stick out and he gripped it and they pulled him to the bank where he lay, weeds about his legs and hair. It reminded me of the day Jimmy drowned.

His breath subsided. Slowly, he stood and began to walk over the fields back to the school. They ran after him with his pullover and pants and shirt but he didn't acknowledge them. I caught the Owl's eye. He looked at me, his expression sad, like the dog Laika's in the spaceship. Then something hard came into his eyes, like he knew somehow I had betrayed him.

❧

At nights in the seminary, I used to look from the dormitory windows out to the motorway in the distance and dream of a seaside town only two hours away. We'd been brought there once, on a day trip, by the priests. Farther away, beyond the woods, the windows of the London-bound train flashed by in lighted silence. London.

I thought of the sea town in class or chapel or as I lay awake in my thin bed, the seeds of doubt growing about this vocation to be a priest. To spend a solitary life without someone to love, ending your days like poor old Father Burke, talking to himself in the presbytery garden.

Hell was losing its power to frighten me and Heaven its ability to comfort. I no longer found meaning in the chapel hymns and prayers, though I still loved the words and melodies. I imagined other lives beyond this suffocating place. The priests had warned me that the Devil whispers in the ear of a doubting Thomas, tempting him with dangerous thoughts.

During our free hour before class, a few mates and I would sneak out to the graveyard with one of the seniors, whom we called the Commie, to smoke Wild Woodbine or Park Drive cigarettes. We would sit on the tomb of a fellow who had died many years before, and talk about sex and music and football and the outside world. I envied the Commie his passionate convictions and his knowledge, skepticism, and certainty about everything.

One morning he told us he'd read that Stalin once studied to be a priest and lost his faith when he challenged God to show himself if He existed, and cursed Him when only silence answered. Stalin knew in his heart that there was no God and no Devil, either, therefore no sin and no punishment. There was no next world.

—Religion is a fairy tale, the Commie said, to give people easy answers to the most complex questions of life, and religion is the opium of the people. Keeps them quiet so they don't ask too many questions. Why would anyone pray to a madman from a thousand years ago who lived up a tree and ate only berries brought to him by his lunatic followers? Why do we believe the ignorant ravings of what Bronze Age nomads thought about the world?

I was longing for a new life. How much longer could I endure the dawn bell rudely awakening the sleeping dormitories, the priest walking among the beds, prodding us into life? My feet on the cold floor, trooping with the others to the washrooms. Holding out hands and nails for inspection, like children. Days of routine, prescribed by bells and study and prayers.

Some of us were afraid to leave because of shame—that we would be regarded as failures or disappointments to our families, especially our mothers who believed that a priest in the house is a gift from God.

But I had had enough of being told what to think, which books I could read, what I could watch and listen to, and of being spied upon day and night. In the library, I devoured books. I was looking for myself, and for answers to my life. Tales of gangsters, explorers, teddy bears, or ballet dancers; lives of painters and footballers, I was indiscriminate in my appetite.

I read poetry too, which fired my imagination of other worlds. The highwayman riding up to the old inn door where Bess the landlord's black-eyed daughter waits, plaiting a love knot in her long black hair; "The Listeners," about a traveler knocking on a moonlit door as ghosts within the old house listen "to that voice from the world of men." And every night I would watch the London train flash through the distant trees.

One day, a notice appeared on the board outside the breakfast room. A theater troupe was coming to present a play, and for weeks it was all the fellows talked about.

At Christmas and on feast days, we had put on our own skits and concerts and sometimes musicals, but this would be a real play with real actors from the outside world. On the night of the performance the rector addressed us from the stage about good manners and respect for the performers who had so generously agreed to give of their time to entertain us. His words were drowned by stomping feet.

—We want the play! We want the play! we all chanted in unison.

The curtain opened to reveal the London flat of the hero, where men with mustaches and monocles were discussing a murder in clipped accents. It felt as though I was watching a dream. There was a stillness inside me as if I were under a spell.

An actress entered dressed in a gaberdine coat over pale legs, her hair lustrous in the surreal light of the stage. In the play she was called Marjorie. We all leaned toward her to be nearer.

She sat on the sofa and crossed her legs, her dress riding up to show her nylons. She held a cigarette between her fingers. Her voice was hoarse. Light caressed her body as if she was a painting come to life. I could not take my eyes from her.

At the end, the actors bowed and she stepped forward toward us, touching her thighs with her hands.

Later, I opened the window to watch the actors board their bus. I saw her move along the pathway, dressed now in skirt and beret. Did she turn toward me and blow a kiss? Yes, she did.

Not to all the fellows hanging from the dormitory windows wolf-whistling and waving, calling to her. No, it was to me, to me alone.

I lay down, restless, and later went again to the window and waited for the lights of the London train to pass in the distance.

~~~⌾⌾⌾~~~

Then the Commie was gone, without saying goodbye. He had been expelled, cited as a bad influence on his fellow seminarians with his sacrilegious ideas.

Myself and the others left behind were on the tomb beneath the yew trees having a smoke one morning after mass when a priest appeared from the bushes. They had been monitoring me for months, my incessant breaking of rules, my disrespect for authority. But especially my friendship with the expelled Commie who had led so many astray.

The rector told me to pack my bags.

A taxi from the village came to bring me to the train. I took a last look at the great house with its flaking paint which had been my home for four years, the football field where I had been happiest. *Come train quickly! Take me away!*

On board I was greedy for every new sight, smoking Woodbines and no one to stop me in the swaying corridor as the landscape flashed by. The rhythm of the train, heartbeat of steel on steel; lovers kissing on a platform as we sped past. A screech of brakes and we stopped; distant voices from other carriages; across from me a man in a cardigan who looked like my father sighed and folded his newspaper over a photograph of the Beatles to read the racing section. The chip-chirp of birds as wind moved the ivy on the redbrick walls of the station. The face of a bathing beauty smiled at me. *Get away to beautiful Torquay.* The beginning of plowed fields, the spire of a church, a manor house, a cluster of small cottages. The rusted sculpture of an abandoned factory. Fires on the embankments even in those early April days. Children flew a kite on a hill. Shadows raced across the fields and startled cattle running. At last the sea like a big blue blanket you could pull over yourself; boats on stilts waiting for the tide; the modesty-preserving beach huts; a boy looking for worms or shells way out there on the sands. A dog mad with sea joy. The colors of houses sea blues and pink, the grey of Birmingham forgotten.

I ran down the slopy road to the harbor. In the distance, farty trombones and trumpets of a brass band; on the seafront, women clutching handbags gazed out to sea. Signs for peppered mackerel, winkles and cockles. And there it was: the old theater where they had brought us to see a variety show. I stood outside the planked-up doors; long-ago laughter trapped inside with the ghosts of little Johnny Trunley, the Fat Boy of Peckham, Winnie Atwell and her laughing piano. And the ghostly voice of the master of ceremonies. *This time, ladies and gentlemen, chiefly yourselves. All together now.*

Down the wooden steps onto the beach I ran.

Now look at me. Belting over sunlit sands, my cries of joy borne on the wind, my spirit freed from its cage at last, inhaling deep into myself the smell of salt and blessed freedom, all my newborn life before me.

I RETURNED TO DUBLIN a failed priest in the spring of my fifteenth year. My mother and father worried themselves over me.

—What are you going to with your life? You can't spend your days lying a hull in the bed.

—If a bomb exploded under the bed he'd just turn over and go back to sleep. No job. No prospects. What in the name of God is going to become of him?

—And now the latest is he's thinking of joining the army.

—Sure what army would have him. Too lazy to scratch himself. Has to be dug out of the bloody billiard hall smoking like a chimney with all the other layabouts and corner boys.

—I caught him trying to sneak in through the back window in the kitchen. Standing there and the smell of drink off him would knock a horse down.

—See where that will land him.

—Yes, in a motorbike helmet above in the mental hospital banging his head off the wall with all the other wet brains.

—Learn a trade, a trade will always stand to you.

I was apprenticed to a firm of plumbers and central-heating engineers. Central heating was becoming all the rage. There was an advertisement for it on television. A camera moved along a row of houses. In the sitting room of the first house we saw a shivering, miserable-looking family in front of a coal fire. In the next we saw a happy smiling father, mother beaming with their children on the sofa, because they had central heating. *The Brady's are the wise ones*, a voice-over said.

—Fuck them and their central heating, I shouted at the television. I resented and detested this family beyond reason as I detested the Hollywood Brady family.

Hi Mom. Hi Dad.

Hi Greg. Sleep well?

Hey you guys, can we have a meeting about my date this evening?

A meeting about his date? Did kids say things like this to their parents?

A maid served them orange juice.

This happy, well-adjusted bunch and their happy teeth. Could there be families like this in the world?

I was a dreadful plumber. On winter mornings with the cold of the pipes in claustrophobic cellars I knew this was not my calling.

—How the fuck did he get in here, he's as useless as a eunuch in a harem. He's the worst I've come across in forty years, I overheard Tommy, an emphysemic plumber say.

They thought I was a danger to myself and the other men.

We traveled to jobs in a springless van that was falling apart with rust, and I listened to their tales of toilets and legendary plumbers.

—Y'know the big building at the end of Nassau Street? Tommy here put in the plumbing there. A master. That man is the Picasso of toilets.

To try to become one of them, I would buy the tabloid papers every morning and make lewd comments about the barebreasted girls on page three. They ate their sandwiches away from me. I felt a failure—a failed plumber and priest.

A stooped sleeveen of a man who managed the yard one day asked if he could have a word.

—Ever noticed the little van that pulls up at the back door on Friday afternoons? You know the bloke who drives it? Sometimes he might need a hand to take away stuff. Extra stuff. You get my drift? You get two pounds a week here, right? I bet you could do with a few extra quid!

I remembered Jemser, the humpbacked thief who lived near us.

Always watching. Like a tiger waiting to pounce.

Light-finger money out of your pocket without you even knowing.

A cockstrutting humpyback with an Elvis quiff and a blue waistcoat with flowers on it, Moroccan blade secreted. And his redheaded girl with the gammy eye scouring the crowds for wallets and purses and whatever else they could get. She, slithering through windows to open the door for him, like Oliver Twist.

—And we divvy up fifty-fifty, fair and square. Nobody messes with us.

—Give you a laugh, he told me: we dressed up as nuns once, robbed a jewelry shop, made off with a trayful of rings. Still the guards can't catch us, dopey fucks, even though we've robbed half the houses of the city.

In the picture house one night, he cut the back of a lad's camel coat in the dark.

—Threatening to squeal on us, the runty fuck. Never felt a thing until he stood up and half his coat fell off in a neat square, and there was me and me bird, smiling at him as if butter wouldn't melt. *What?* says I to him. *What are you looking at, Bollicky Bill?*

I thought that maybe being a thief like Jemser wouldn't be a bad way to live.

I would give up a pound to my mother from my wages, leaving it on the mantelpiece in a brown pay envelope like my father did. I paid weekly for my racing bike with ten gears and drop handles. My father hated this bike, thought I was going to be killed on it. He didn't know that I'd forged his name as guarantor. I would ride all over the city, weaving in and out of traffic, sometimes with no hands or holding onto the backs of trucks or with my feet on the handlebars.

On summer evenings I cycled into the mountains or out to the sea at Howth, movie themes playing in my head. I was saving for a suit from Burton's of Dame Street, a navy blue, thin-lapeled, mohaired job with a white shirt and desert boots that would transform me into Michael Caine. I dreamed of girls who would be impressed that I had a trade, maybe I'd have my own van and shop one day. With the extra money, I could pay off the bike, buy the mohair suit, and open one of those savings accounts in the post office. Just for lifting a bit of gear into a van.

On Friday evenings, George would reverse into the bay behind the shop. A cigarette hung from his mouth. He went to the rear of the truck, opened the door, and nodded to me.

—Nice day, you got anything for me? His eyes roamed around the warehouse.

The gear to be moved had been marked with a small black cross. I would climb into the forklift and place the fork under the first batch and load it into the van. That's all it took. George would place ten crisp notes in my hand and be gone.

I began to take more risks and soon I owned three mohair suits and several shirts and desert boots and I had my sights set on a Mini Cooper, which I was able to buy within a year. Red, with tan interior and radio, soon it was parked outside our house on the pavement for all to see and envy.

Then a manager approached me one day to have a word.

—We know what you're at. If it was up to me, you'd be in jail. You're a fucking thick shite doing their dirty work. Not only are you a useless apprentice, you're a stupid thief as well.

The getup of you strutting around in mohair suits like you're in a bleeding James Bond film. You think I'm as green as I'm cabbage that I wouldn't notice? Now get the fuck out of here and if I ever see your mug around this place I'll have the law on you. The only reason I haven't is because I respect your father, a decent, hardworking man.

I spent my days haunting the picture houses and billiard halls when I wasn't tramping all over the city looking for work. I needed money. My brother Tom was a chef in a hotel in the center of the city. He gave me a job washing dishes.

—Scrub everything that comes over here. Here's your bucket for swill, here's the sink, here's your hose. Make sure you get all the gunk off and leave everything spic and span.

He handed me a brown coat which was sizes too big and reached down to my shoes.

—Jesus, I said.

—Just roll the sleeves up. Nobody's going to see you. You're a fucking dishwasher.

The kitchen was like the engine room of a ship. A cauldron of shouting, cursing, and sweating. In a small office to the side was the head chef, a huge German who came out now and then to taste what was on the stove. I wanted to do well for my brother's sake. I scrubbed like a demon and got into a rhythm, and time passed in a blur of grease cleaning, floor mopping, and whistling.

I became aware of the German chef shouting as the kitchen went quiet.

—Where is the cauliflower? His words echoed as if he was shouting down a well.

Tom rushed over to me. His face was a panic.

—Where's the fucking cauliflower? There's 150 people out there for a wedding with mouths on them waiting for their cauliflower.

The German was barely able to breathe.

—It's not really his fault, my brother said to him.

—I was told to wash everything, chef.

—He has thrown out ze cauliflower for ze wedding. Ziss is a fucking disaster. Get him out of my kitchen.

I handed my long brown coat to another lad who was already at the sink.

And that is how I became a toilet attendant at a major Dublin hotel.

♦

It was around this time that I met my first serious girlfriend at the local dance hall.

She mercifully stood and followed me into the lurching couples for the slow dance because I couldn't jive or twist. My arm encircled her waist, touched the bone of her hip, and my hand felt the bra strap beneath her blouse; her hair brushed my face, her hand rested on my shoulder, and the soft hills of her breasts pressed against me. Looking out over her head, she looking at the other dancers, *Would she rather be with some other bloke?* I thought.

Words whirled like leaves madly stirred by a wind inside my head; bodies closer now and I fought to keep my man from rising.

Think of something awful. Remember the time you saw the crash at the crossroads and the dead girl's face covered in blood staring at you so that you couldn't sleep for months; but even conjuring up the dead girl didn't put manners on this thing in my trousers that ruled my life with a mind of his own. It's a terrible plight to be a boy with this thing growing out of you giving away the dirty game you're at.

She tilted her face to me and offered her mouth with eyes closed and I bent to the softness of her lips, and because I had practiced so often on my own hand, I knew how to do it gently.

I felt her respond and we both hung there on each other's lips until the music ended and she pulled away and thanked me, waiting for me to ask her again, and then we slow danced for an eternity of hours after which I said:

—I'll walk you home.

I didn't care where she lived, as long as I could just walk with her. She collected her coat and I waited outside on the steps smoking, and then at last she appeared. Outside in new light she looked pale.

She hooked my arm, leaned in against me going over the bridge. I loved the voice of her and the way she was just a little smaller than me. *Maybe this could be true love*, I thought.

She talked about her job in a meat export office and her favorite singers.

—I love Gene Pitney too, I lied.

After a long time, we reached her house.

I kissed her and forgot about the dead girl in the accident because she didn't seem to mind the bulge throbbing like a mad thing against her. My hand moved to her breast, her breath heavy in my ear.

Then a voice called her name. A man in a vest with a clock in his hand stood in the doorway.

—It's my father, I better go in.

—Meet at the dance hall, at the bandstand again next week, I said, and then stood and watched her leave, the light going off downstairs, her shadow against the window, and I hoped she would look out, yet she didn't.

I thought of her undressing, lying there under the bedclothes, and wondered if she was also thinking of those deepening kisses before her father appeared, tongues searching, quickening breath, wordless acquiescence to go further.

It was a long walk home, but my feet had wings like in the song, bearing me happily to my own sleeping street.

I counted the minutes until I'd see her again. I was addicted to her, I couldn't sleep. I pitied people who weren't us. We made each other laugh and we both felt we understood the other completely. Yet I felt I was hiding my greatest faults where I believed she had none. The thought of her sustained me. I would daydream about her face, her body. Her smile, her touch.

We would sit in my car and talk for hours. There was nothing about her that didn't fascinate me. We invented words around our private world. I'd imitate people, even her father, to make her laugh. When I called for her I was shown into the good sitting room and he always came in and sat opposite me in his armchair. He'd begin talking about football but soon he'd be onto the stories of his life in the country years ago, eating raw turnips in the fields, and how the only toys they had were a stick and a bicycle tire. How the youth of today didn't know how lucky they were to have what they had. And about all the promiscuity and the pill and drugs and students gone mad in the streets protesting about the war in Vietnam.

—And sure half the time you can't tell a girl from a boy with the long hair on them and the tight trousers. Where is it all going to end? The world is gone mad. Oh now, don't be paying attention to me. I'm just an old goat.

Then one night most unexpectedly we had our first row. My jealousy was the cause. She was talking to a friend of mine at a party.

—Did you have to be so amused by his stupid jokes? And the way you were looking at each other—it's so obvious you fancy him. She told me I was paranoid and childish.

—Grow up, she said.

We said awful things but then, devastated, I begged her to forgive me. We made up and swore we'd never argue again. I surprised her with a box of After Eight mints in the glove compartment. I bought her a bottle of perfume, and she dabbed it behind her ear and kissed me. And she told me, *I love you.*

But then we began to disagree over things we had always agreed on. She hinted at engagement, and one night before the main feature at the Savoy Cinema there was an advertisement for a jeweler's. She suddenly became pouty and at last revealed that she desperately wanted to get married. Engagement was the beginning of a life I hadn't really thought about. Marriage, children, a mortgage.

—It's not what I want. I don't want anything to change between us, I told her.

—You don't love me, she said.

After that, her silences were more frequent and impenetrable. We always seemed to be bickering. We took each other for granted and sex had lost the mad excitement of the early days. We didn't look in each other's eyes like we used to. I began to think what life would be like with someone else, and I wondered if she was thinking the same.

When she wasn't with me, my jealousy grew. I became moody and withdrawn. I began to find fault with things I had loved before: her laugh was too loud when we were with friends, she cracked her knuckles too much.

I had decided we should break up but I couldn't bear the thought of her being with someone else. And I didn't want to be lonely again.

One day she said:

—Let's do something crazy. Let's take a week off work, pretend to be sick, and go to Paris. We'll go to a bar and pretend we don't know each other and you can chat me up.

Now I was thinking of the right time to end it.

What if I picked an argument in the pub or maybe did it over the phone? What if we broke up and then I changed my mind—would she take me back again? I agonized over what to say.

But then it happened when I least expected it. She told me it wasn't me. I was the most wonderful person she'd ever met. That I'd be happier with someone else.

We had our last kiss in a taxi home. The driver turned his radio a little louder as if he knew.

I walked her to the door and she turned on the steps. For all the words I might have said, no words came. A passing siren drowned out her words and she did not repeat them. I stood by the garden gate willing her to look back one last time. But the door closed behind her. I waited for the light in her room to come on but it stayed dark. I made my way along the empty street and bade goodbye to us.

One random day months later, I ran into a mutual friend. I asked how she was, polite and casual.

—Oh, she said, same as usual. Happy-go-lucky. You know how she is. She cut her hair.

I had always loved her hair, and now I remembered that room in Wexford where we'd gone the one weekend, in a cheap guesthouse that smelled of frying and floor polish.

—Let me brush out your hair, I'd asked. Facing the mirror, her eyes closed, she had tilted her head back, surrendering.

I bade goodbye to our mutual friend, and then the old pain came again. I had been in remission for months. Until that mention of her I thought the truth of love had forever fled. Now it invaded again. I could see her smiling in a mirror at some stranger, her silver brush in his hand and she surrendering as once she had to me, secrets and shared laughter commingling.

My friends told me that I should stop moping. That I was a sad sack.

—You think sitting there in the pub is going to bring her back. She's gone. Like the snow of last winter.

—Stop with the jealousy. And stop with the phone calls and the hanging up. She knows it's you.

—Take the hump off your back. Lay down your bag of rocks.

So the days passed into weeks and the weeks into months, and gradually she too faded until many years later when I came across a photograph of us together on a hillside in Greece, our only holiday. A photograph I'd long forgotten tumbled from its envelope carrying the perfume of her after all those years. That perfume! It would be on the pillow, on my shirt, in every room. Now I breathed it in and was back among the cypresses of a monastery in Greece. We had walked for hours to the garden above the sea. We were given minted honey and yogurt and cool retsina by a young monk. Evening came and it was time to return to the hotel. She asked if we could stay in the monastery and the young monk said yes. And in an ancient stone cell, she fell asleep. I lay awake listening to her soft breathing. A bone in her foot cracked. A tiny cry in the throat. Even the chanting of the monks in the early morning did not wake her.

And now there was only this photograph, the ghost of her smiling at me in the shade of cypress trees.

∽◌◌◌◌∽

I had failed at or been fired from so many jobs. Then I tried being a door-to-door encyclopedia salesman, and was trained by a man from Wisconsin.

Twenty of us gathered in Jury's Hotel, where, in his strange American accent, Mr. Combover instructed us in the art of selling books to the housewives of the Dublin suburbs and in how to develop a charismatic personality even if you didn't have one. Not how to be a salesman but how to act the role of the salesman. He had the mad zeal of a Redemptorist preacher.

—Keep your body and voice relaxed! Maintain eye contact! Ask permission to use a name. Like this: *May I call you Mrs. Gilhooley?* Never interrupt and if you do, apologize: *I'm sorry, Mrs. Gilhooley, you were saying?* Acknowledge questions with enthusiasm: *I'm so glad you asked me that, Mrs. Gilhooley.* Never bring your personal mood with you, no matter what's happening in your life. Believe in what you are doing because if you don't, the buyer will not. You will be rejected every day but you will not allow that to discourage you. Rejection is hardly ever personal in this business. Unless it is. Out of ten wives, five might close the door, three will be undecided, and two will be buyers. The customer is not always right—she can be talked into or out of anything. Learn to listen. That's hard for you guys, being Irish, I know.

We pretended this was funny.

—You have to be likeable, and if you're not, you have to act being likeable. If you are shy and not confident, act the opposite. No looking in windows, stand politely back from the door.

—What about dogs? I have a phobia about dogs, I said.

—Let them smell your hand, said Mr. Combover.

—What if he bites me first?

—You get a tetanus shot.

A handsome chap called Billy and me set off into the suburbs. Mr. Combover had us all get haircuts, short back and sides, and shave our beards because beards had suspicious implications. Leather jackets ditto.

—We look like Mormon missionaries, I said.

We took lunch in the pub, toasted cheese in cellophane, a bowl of instant soup, and a pint. All we talked about was sex, films, and football. Billy was a Manchester United fan like me, and George Best, the world's greatest footballer, was from near where he lived in Belfast. He told me about his life growing up there, Catholics and Protestants living in fear of each other and the bitter hatred between them.

—People in the South haven't a clue and they don't care, even though there is a war going on two hours up the road.

Billy's parents wanted him to go to university to study law at Queens, but what he really wanted was to be was an actor in London.

On fine days we went out to Sandymount Strand to watch the girls sunbathing. Billy talked about his dreams of acting one day with the Royal Shakespeare Company.

—I like this selling lark. It's good training for my acting, he would say.

We worked well as partners, and I could see how great an actor he might be. We were invited into houses to sit on floral sofas and listen to women who often revealed intimacies we found exciting. Billy would make them laugh and they found his northern accent attractive.

—You remind me of Robert Redford, one said.

—Butch and Sundance, that's us, I said, hoping I'd remind her of Paul Newman.

One offered us wine, even though it was only ten in the morning. Billy gave me the secret signal to make myself scarce. The venetian blinds snapped shut in the upstairs room and twenty minutes later, Billy came down the garden path whistling softly and straightening his tie. (*Nobody buys from a tieless salesman!*)

It was the first job I liked. Maybe because Billy and I were acting.

I returned to school and secured a scholarship to university. The first of the family ever to get to third level.

—You have the brains, wherever you got them. I left school when I was twelve, my father said.

They never guessed how I thought about my time at university. It was like an extension of school. Like waiting for a flight in an airport for four years. In that place of concrete I felt like I did not exist corporeally. I was a kind of ectoplasm. I was bored by the professors on the podium, gowns wrapped self-importantly about them. Then exam time when the year's furious scribbling of lectures, bland as frozen dinners, were regurgitated back to the examining board.

I'd believed university would inspire me with a love for knowledge and learning. Instead I felt condescended to, indoctrinated with unquestioned ideas. Theory was valued over experience, the fictitious past superior to the reality of the present. I learned without passion, and I was still an outsider. Still blushing. Desperately shy. And so lonely. I had wanted to join the university drama group but lost my nerve when I was called to audition for a nonspeaking part in an Ionesco play.

There were parties in damp flats, stoner music leaking mournfully through curtains, carryouts from pubs after closing time, up creaking stairs past landladies on red alert. Student longhairs like myself in army coats; would-be writers who read Ferlinghetti and Camus and drunkenly discussed existentialism and revolution. Girls with legs mottled by single-bar heaters, on scholarships from country convents, rolled joints with delicate fingers, posters of Horslips and Hendrix on their walls, tights drying on bathroom rails. Sex in single beds that sagged in the middle, sweat and semen stains on the nylon sheets.

Vietnam, American imperialism, the Brits, the North, the destruction of the city by barbarian developers, exploitation by the capitalist philistines. We marched and linked arms in protest:

fuck the church, fuck politicians, and the whole fucking hypo-critical system.

On graduation day, the president waited with my scroll. My name was called and I stepped forward to receive my degree. My parents stood beside me, awkward and proud. My father in his Sunday suit, his leather belt holding up his trousers. My mother in a straw hat and a blue suit.

—That's you. That's your name, said my mother. Go on up before he gives it to someone else.

MY DEPRESSION, it seems, was often linked to my drinking.

—Alcohol is the cause of half the world's misery. The same bloody Arthur Guinness and his little yellow brother, John Jameson.

I had an uncle who apparently drank away two farms and a lorry. My father drank. Sometimes we looked out the window waiting for him to be on the last bus. And then would begin the vigil in my mother's bedroom, praying he would arrive safely home. When we heard footsteps on the pavement, my mother would ask:

—Is it him?

I started young. I remember Christmas morning of my eighth year. There had been a glass of whiskey on top of the piano, and our neighbor, a huge man who had trouble breathing, held the glass to the light, then swirled its contents around in his mouth before he swallowed. The firelight shone in its yellow liquid; I watched him like a dog watching a rabbit.

—Jaysus, he said, low groans coming out of him.

—That's a man can drink, said my father.

Later someone gave me a sup from a glass of porter. It tasted bitter and I shivered as I swallowed but even then, even though it tasted like medicine, I wanted more. They pulled the glass away from me.

—He's a divil for the drink, they said, laughing.

The chapel was my first theater.

I loved the music of Latin words, the sudden river of light through stained glass windows, when clouds made way for sun, as if God's blessings were pouring in on us all.

I loved to breathe in the aroma of fresh flowers, especially lilac for the month of Mother Mary in May. Even the musk of lily in the mortuary, where at night the dead lay alone in varnished coffins.

It was a place of comfort, full of stories and drama.

Christ's body hung on the cross, a cloth covering his nakedness, His sad eyes turned to His Father's Heaven, bone-broken and in despair. All this He had suffered for our sins, that we might be redeemed and have life eternal, we were told.

All that suffering for me and the sinners of Dublin and the whole world made me feel guilty. I would never ask God to do that.

The stations of the cross were like frozen scenes of a film. The story of Christ's last journey to Golgotha Hill to be crucified, stumbling along the Via Dolorosa, falling down three times under the sticks and whips of the soldiers; Veronica, her arms outstretched, with a towel to wipe the blood from his face. His mother weeping beneath the cross. All of it deeply moved my child's mind.

Candles flickered for good intentions before the saints in the side chapels. The favorite in our parish was St. Francis, once a no-good boyo, who gave away all his possessions to poor people.

—So mark that well, my mother said, you who can't even give a lick of an ice pop to your brother without a sulk puss on you.

St. Anthony, the patron saint of lost things, was opposite holding a fat baby Jesus.

—Well, missus, I looked high up and low down and, in the end, I said a prayer to St. Anthony. Of course, there it was stuck behind the wardrobe. He must be driven mental with people praying to him day and night for wallets and car keys.

St. Jude was the saint of hopeless causes, the last stop before disaster, but he passed a lot of his cases on to St. Anthony.

And there were always little plays to be part of. Mass, confession, benediction, the May procession with the Virgin carried through the streets, everyone singing and praying the rosary.

In Lent, red flannel and two candles were laid across your throat by the priest to prevent serious illness, but it didn't cover a sore throat, which might get you a day off school.

On Good Friday at three o'clock the sky was supposed to darken because that was the time our Lord died. When it didn't, Father Burke said it wasn't the Irish three o'clock but the time in Calvary in the Holy Land.

Easter Sunday the chapel was bright with candles and flowers, and choirs sang hymns of joy.

—If we live good lives we will live forever and ever in Heaven with God the Father who protects us and loves us although we are sinners, but you must live never committing any sin. Or you will end up burning in the fires of Hell for all time, said the brother.

He explained eternity to us by holding a lighted match under a boy's finger and made us all repeat together:

—Forever and ever and ever and ever and ever and ever and ever and ever . . . till the word lost all meaning and the pain made the boy dance, howling across the floor.

—To burn for ever and ever in a pit with all the other howling sinners.

But the worst pain isn't being on fire for all time. It is to be deprived of the sight of the face of God and the chance to dwell with Him for eternity in His Father's mansion.

If you stole money from your mother's purse or told lies or had impure thoughts about Mary Wheelan's pink knickers, which you saw the day she fell off the wall into the bushes, you'd have go to Hell and be roaring in pain for all of eternity.

God lived in the tabernacle on the main altar, which could be opened only with a golden key which the priest took from inside his altar clothes, which were like a woman's frock but you could always see his own men's shoes sticking out from beneath the lace.

When I was a child, I thought Jesus had a bed or a sofa and chairs in a little sitting room in the tabernacle.

Altar boys attended the priest with their oiled hair and holy faces. I envied them their proximity to the golden house where Jesus lived and all the secrets of the altar drama they knew.

The priest bowed to them during the mass. What a strange thing that was, a grown-up bowing to a boy.

I saw them make their way to the sacristy for the morning masses, carrying leather bags like miniature doctors on important business.

I wanted more than anything to become one of them.

I learned cues for when and how to cross the steps of the altar, how to genuflect before the tabernacle, how to ring the small bell for the consecration with decisive notes. I learned not to make eye contact with the congregation, never to smile or acknowledge friends or family, to always be respectful and involved so the congregation believed in what we were doing, serving the holy sacraments.

—Make sure your laces are tied, the brother warned, not like the lad who tripped and fell on the marble steps and had to be ferried to hospital with a broken nose and split lip.

After weeks of preparation I was ready to be tested before Father Burke, who sat before me on the altar in the echoing chapel. I had never walked on a carpet before and it was soft as a cloud.

The priest's face was reflected in the brass plate commemorating the Eucharistic Congress, and he was beating out the rhythm of the responses with his cane along with me. He looked bored and scratched like a dog under his chin.

—I cannot abide a mumbler, he said. Every word must be heard and understood, even in the back of the chapel. Mean what you say. Listen for your cues. Don't talk over me. Never make me have to repeat myself. And attend to those hideous stumps, he said, examining my bitten nails.

I want neck washed, hair cut, shoes polished, trousers pressed, clean shirt, spick and span. You'll report to Mr. Comerford, the sacristan, seven a.m. Monday morning. Do not be late.

The night before the morning of the first mass I slept on and off. My throat was dry, stomach heaving with panic. I felt driven by a new excitement. Time seemed to bend each moment into an hour, yet each hour was a moment. The sacristan, whose ears were stopped with cotton wool to prevent some class of a green slime leaking out, brought me to an anteroom behind the altar that smelled of stale incense. I could hear the congregation filling the chapel.

The other boys had an easy familiarity, horse-playing with each other.

They pulled on the great rope to ring the final bell which called out over the streets, and it pulled them up to the ceiling, the wind blowing their soutanes comically out. I had heard this bell every day of my life calling the people to mass, or reminding them to stop what they were doing and cross themselves at the noon hour, and at six in the evening for the Angelus.

In my vestments of white lace with the cross and lamb and black soutane beneath, I presented my fingernails for inspection, my ears were checked for dirt, my hair was plastered down with Brylcreem.

We helped the priest to dress. His white alb was tied with a cord at the waist; after, a stole was crossed and tucked into the cord. He bent his head into the outer vestment. He took the chalice given to him on the day of my ordination by my parents, looked at himself one last time in the mirror.

We moved from the sacristy into the hushed and crowded chapel and before the congregation, who stood to greet our entrance.

I stepped with fearful solemnity onto that stage for the first time. It felt like opening the door of a hot oven. I felt absolutely present yet floating outside myself as if I were another person altogether.

I fell in with a boy called Clukko, twice suspended from serving mass for misconduct, who was in what Mr. Comerford called "the last chance saloon."

We were smoking in the belfry, looking out over the roads and the houses to the hills beyond.

—Likes his sup of wine during the mass, old Father Devlin. Hardly touches the water. Have you noticed? Clukko said.

—Do you think a priest can make wine turn into God's blood like they say?

—Who knows? But the wine is rotgut from Findlater's in North Frederick Street. They get it delivered in cases. I always nick a bottle for myself.

I began to think about wine, and saliva came into my mouth even at the tender age of ten.

I poured it over the priest's fingers into the chalice during mass and watched him swirl it, holding the stem and slowly decanting it into his throat. Against the gold, it seemed even more red and lovely.

Part of my job for the mass was to pour the wine into small glasses called cruets from one of the bottles in the sacristy cabinet. I twisted off the cap and filled them to just below the brim, but once by accident the liquid splashed on my hand and I licked it, tasting its dull flavor. I took a swig from the bottle. After a few minutes, I began to feel joyful as it spread through me, warming all my insides. Soon I too was replacing what I took with water, like Clukko. We stole a bottle now and then, drank it in the field behind the factory. I washed my mouth out with my father's aftershave.

The ten o'clock mass was always sparsely attended because of Father Simpson, the stammering priest who took hours to get through it.

Clukko and I had drawn the short straw for that week and were his servers. We were drifting in and out of attention, answering by rote as we did mostly now, except with Father Devlin, who would swoop down on you like a hawk and give you a clout on your ear hole. Before the mass we had finished a bottle between us up in the belfry.

I knew I was drunk. I heard myself sighing loudly, desperately trying to focus and speak the responses normally, though it felt like I was chewing wool. I rose unsteadily to serve the wafer, staggered on the steps, grabbing for the altar cloth. Sacred vessels, candles, chalice, and book of scripture in its golden cover followed as I tumbled onto the marble floor, landing in a heap. Sour vomit sprayed from my mouth before I passed out.

On the way to school one day I saw a man lying in the door-way of the bookies, a long snake of piss beneath him. I would see him many times after, always alone, sometimes with cuts on his face. They wouldn't let him in the public house to drink because he never had any money and was always get-ting into fights. He was called a drunkard, a strange word, the worst thing a person could be because it meant they wouldn't have a shoe on their foot or a penny to their name. It meant you were a man with no name lying in a doorway with trem-bling hands.

If a man drank too much, or sometimes a woman, like Mrs. O'Moore, they would have to go away to a monastery for a "dry-ing out." When they came home, they would have taken a pledge that they would never ever drink again and would wear a badge in the shape of a heart to warn people not to tempt them by offer-ing them any drink.

—Doesn't touch a drop, only a mineral to pass himself in company. Wild horses wouldn't get him to enter a public house.

Mr. Murphy didn't drink for a year and he loved to tell everyone how he was a new man now, more get-up-and-go, was playing golf, learning Gaelic, and had joined a choir.

—Don't know myself! I'm a new man. Drinking is for the birds.

At Christmas midnight mass, he showed up blind drunk and shouted at the priest. He started to sing "A Nation Once Again" and was roaring, *Up the republic!* before he was bundled out. The next day he went off for another dry out.

Whenever the grown-ups had parties, they laughed a lot and sang and made a fuss of us and gave us money. Sometimes they shouted at each other or got sad when they sang.

If you ever go across the sea to Ireland,
Then maybe at the closing of your day—

—Hey, what are you crying for? You are in Ireland, you clown.

The men would go to the pub in the evenings to get out of the house. Sometimes they brought their wives on Friday or Saturday nights, a gin for her and a pint for him, and there might be a bit of a singsong, and it would be a roaring madhouse with sweating bartenders by ten o'clock. Then the barman would drive them all out.

—Have youse no homes to go to? The guards will be in on top of me and I may wave goodbye to me license. Come on now, last orders.

Then there'd be more singing back in someone's house.

—Shh! A bit of reverence for the singer now.

—O jaysus, not "The Rocks of Bawn."

—Can't believe he's going to inflict this on us. There's two hundred bleedin' verses.

—Go up with that eejit before he pisses into the fire.

—Don't wake the children, for the love of God.

—Take care he doesn't fall down the stairs and break his neck.

I longed to be one of them and have no school but go to work instead, where I would get a brown envelope with money in it called wages. I wanted to be a man and have a gargle with the men at the bar counter, pints in their hands, stomachs straining over belts, the barman knowing me and what my poison was because I was a regular.

Drink was the ruination of the country; the priests railed against it. Even Father Hickey fell prey to it, was arrested for being drunk and disorderly and biting a policeman on the nose. After I was thrown off the altar, my mother had said:

—If I ever smell drink on your breath you need never darken this door again. So after I returned from the seminary I drank lemonade as my friends stood around fires in the backfield drinking cider, and they called me a mammy's boy.

—Are you a man or a mouse? Squeak up!

Alright, fuck it, finally. I took the flagon from them, skulled most of it. I felt a fire of power inside myself and I let out a wild roar that made them all laugh.

Later, I was doubled over, vomiting on my shoes. Rather than go home with the smell of drink on me, I slept in the field and awoke hours later, shivering, a blacksmith inside my head pounding my brain with a hammer.

I made an oath that I would never let a drop pass my lips ever, but I could never stop thinking of the smell of alcohol. When I passed a pub, I sometimes opened the door and pretended I was looking for someone—but it was only to breathe in the smell of drink.

I was seventeen years old the first time I got drunk by myself. Although it was well into autumn, the evening light could have been mistaken for a summer's evening. I bought a six-pack of McArdle's and drank it on Howth Head, out of the way of the hill walkers.

Suddenly the eternal dullness of my days shifted to brightest colors, and I had a great love for the world and an excitement about my place in it. I wanted to share myself with everyone, and when the bottles were gone, I wanted more. I found a pub, and as I sat on the stool it was the first time I felt truly myself, at ease, equal to the world which had, up to then, made me feel that I didn't belong in it.

Later I would drink in every city and every town across the world. With famous actors and down-and-outs, I had bottles, glasses of the most expensive wines, or I finished other people's leavings. It was all the same.

Alcohol had become my most trusted friend, before it betrayed me and brought me to my darkest days. One night I fell down in a doorway and lay there shivering in a pool of my own piss until the police woke me. I couldn't speak; I knew only that I had to have another drink.

‿✑⁓✑‿

By the mid-nineties, alcohol had taken a terrible grip. I remember awakening one morning, cursing the sunlight stinging my eyes. My tongue was thick. I was hungry and sickened by the thought of food, but I needed to drink to cure myself, to quell the racing, random thoughts. A hair of the dog, whatever that meant, to restore calm to screaming nerves. I strove to recall where I'd been the night before; despair when nothing after noon took shape. Twelve hours in a blackout: Where had I been? Whom had I met? I moved parts of my body, checking for broken bones and bruises. I reached for the water and tried to hold the shaking glass, afraid my teeth would shatter it.

The slaking of the thirst was almost thrilling—cold liquid on the fire in my throat. I had spent so many days and nights like this, seeking the lonely room or the roaring pub, the bliss of oblivion. The songs sung, arguments begun, the broken glass and vomit and blood. What passed for a life more dead than alive. *Half in love with easeful death*, as the poet said. Roistering and roaring in the streets like my heroes.

Remnants of pizza, upended bottles surrounded me; on my hands and knees I drank the dregs. Then I found—miraculously —unopened whiskey. I gagged as I forced it down. Soon, the fire spread in my chest and the trembling eased, and I could light a cigarette. I cursed not the drink, but reality. Reality was the problem, the isness. There was a groan from under the sheets, and a naked girl emerged.

—Christ, I'm late, she said, panicked, searching for her underwear. I had no idea who she was. I thought she had no idea who I was either, from the way she tried to make sense of me and of where she was. She dressed quickly with her back to me. A bumblebee costume was strewn on the floor, and then I remembered: it was Halloween. We'd met in a pub; I had admired her costume. Mascara was on her cheeks—was she crying? Had I offended her? I recalled something about her saying how lonely she'd been, but that was all I could remember.

—What about your costume? I asked.

—I can't go out dressed like a fucking bee. She asked to borrow an overcoat to get home.

—See you around, she said, backing out the door.

And the place was suddenly empty. I looked over at the bee costume on the floor and was flooded with despair and shame, and anger and remorse, and hatred for who I was. And I decided the best thing was to get drunk again. My body was trembling again, and though my teeth were chattering, sweat poured off me.

I had spilled something on myself; and realized, without surprise, it was blood, which covered the sheets and my clothes. Almost bemusedly in the mirror, I took in the blue and black of my own bruised face. My eye was shut with dried blood, and when I opened my mouth, a tooth hung, comically broken in my gums.

I drew a breath, and a viscous pain enveloped my entire body. I sank to the floor, seeking comfort in the cold tiles. I hoped that this time the eternal bacchanal had ended. But I knew it hadn't. There would be so many days and nights of suffering to come.

Eventually I found the courage to call someone.

—I can't go on dying like this, I told my friend Teri.

—I've known for a long time, she said.

She arranged for me to go to a hospital specializing in alcohol and drug addiction. The following day before I left, although I was still shaking I wanted to have a last drink. In a pub where I wasn't known I ordered a large whiskey. And another. Then gin. But nothing happened. It was early summer. Drinkers stood chatting outside the pub. I envied them their ability to enjoy life. They seemed so at ease with each other. I'd never felt that. Always on the outside looking in.

At the clinic they gave me a sleeping pill. I was exhausted. I just wanted to sleep for weeks. Not have to see or talk to anybody.

—Time to get up, said a nurse the following morning. I brushed my teeth. Nausea rose in my throat.

A sea of people looked up as I entered the breakfast room. Every instinct bade me turn around and flee but I fought it off. I joined a table. A man shook my hand.

—It'll get better, he said.

And it did. Day by day I gained courage. The veils of denial and delusion lifted. I wanted my life back again. With the kindness of my fellow patients and counselors, who encouraged me to be ruthlessly honest with them and especially with myself, I began to see how sick I was, and that the disease of alcoholism was not a moral weakness. I was powerless over it. But I took it one day at a time. Today, I am over twenty years sober.

WHEN MY SISTER MARIAN WAS LITTLE, I used to take her to dance classes. On the bus to Meath Street, up Francis Street, and then to Thomas Street. I would sit outside, listening to the thunder of feet on the floorboards and the Irish cèilidh music. She would come out flushed and happy. On the way home, we'd stop to buy slices of gur cake at a sweetshop. The old woman behind the counter shuffled to and fro, in an overcoat and elastic stockings, disturbed from the backroom where she has been sitting by the fire. Her fingers were swollen from the cold and arthritis. Mrs. Miserable, people called her.

My sister adored me, and we basked in each other's love. She told me all her secrets, like the time the Smiler showed her his thing outside the chipper. She was beautiful, smart, and hilariously funny.

On the cusp of her twenties, in 1972, Marian was first hospitalized.

The phone call came at night. When I answered I heard a polite English voice:

—Mental hospital.

I say the words to myself now and a coldness comes over my body. A stilling of the world around me.

—Who was that? my father asked.

—Nobody.

—How, I thought, am I going to tell my parents that my sister, with her eyes like blue seas, who was more my friend than a sister, has had a breakdown in a London high street?

I flew from Dublin to London and took the train out to a small town in the countryside. A place I had associated with a fourth-division football team.

—Drugs, yes, that's what it is, I told myself. Someone has given her dodgy drugs and she's had a reaction. That's all it is.

When I arrived at the hospital, I had to steel myself against dread. That dreary place, with barred windows, bid no welcome to the world. Birds flew out of its ancient chimneys in fright; patients shuffled in the grounds, smoking; others argued furiously with themselves, laughed at secret things, eyes vacant and haunted.

—Nice day, I said to one.

—What's fucking nice about it?

I put on my visitor's mask to seem normal in the house of the mad.

—Your sister is confined.

That's the word they used. I would have wept right there in the doorway, wouldn't have cared who saw me. I couldn't for her sake. I had to let her see that all was well with the world, that being there was nothing to be anxious about. Just for a few weeks to find the right medication and then she'd be out and would never look back.

There was an after-smell of fried breakfast, which made me want to vomit. Then the silence was split open by awful screams. The nurse with a drinker's flushed face didn't even glance up from his desk. Was I the only one who heard it?

The doctor came squeaking along the corridor dressed not in a white coat but in a tweed jacket, like a teacher. Dead-fish handshake on him. I followed him into an office. On his desk were photos of his children and wife at some ski resort, woolen-hatted. All looking not mad. Normal.

—Your sister has suffered a breakdown, he began. There was an incident. She says she had some kind of religious apparition. Saw something or someone in the sky. We are keeping her calm. She was an emergency admission through the police, who found her in distress on the high street. But this hospital is outside her place of residence, you understand, and so we cannot keep her indefinitely. We shall have to release her into your care as her next of kin. We have arranged a transfer to an Irish hospital where she can continue treatment.

—What is wrong with her? When she left Dublin, she was fine. Is it drugs? LSD maybe?

—Perhaps, he said, looking out the window, where some patients were kicking a ball about.

We entered a room in which a few women sat, one rocking back and forth in front of the television, watching a children's program with a cutout giraffe talking to a duck.

—Give us a cigarette, Mr. Man, she said to me, then went back to rocking.

My sister came toward me, shuffling in paper slippers, food in her hair, fingers brown from nicotine, looking at me as if she didn't know me. We sat at a table as I feigned nonchalance. An omelet was set down before her.

—We don't let them have knives or forks. For their own safety, said the nurse, a big woman with glasses.

It is this which made me want to weep, watching her sitting there, drinking from a plastic container, pulling the food apart, stuffing it into her mouth.

—She doesn't seem to know who I am, I said.

—That's normal.

—Normal?

—The medication, the nurse said.

There was a smell of urine in the airless room. The sun shone through the grille, making a pathway across the floor. A girl my sister's age rolled in it, her flowered dress riding up her white legs. A grey-haired lady was having her hair brushed, another was being walked around by a nurse, her shapeless gown open at the back. There was a scream of rage.

—I'll take your fucking head off and serve it to you on a plate!

—Now, now, Emily, said the nurse firmly. Come over here and color in these pictures. There's a good girl.

Marian asked how her hair was as they had no mirrors. Her mouth was smudged with lipstick. I wet my handkerchief and rubbed it off, and she wriggled away like a child, laughing.

On the train she fell asleep and leaned her head on my shoulder. I didn't want people to think that we were a couple, so I gently moved away from her.

The countryside sped past and gave way to the houses and back gardens of people who knew nothing of madness. A sudden anger erupted inside me. I felt impotent before something awful and inevitable. It reminded me of the time when a menacing dog would not let me pass on a deserted road and I felt paralyzed by fear, and then anger at my own powerlessness.

—Where are we going?

—We are going home, I told her.

—Country roads take me home, she sang to herself.

By the time we reached the airport, a storm was coming. The sky darkened, and there was a downpour as we sat in the lounge. An announcement told us the flight was delayed because of the weather. Indefinitely. Marian shivered, as if trying to shake something off. The stupor of medication was fading. She was alert now, her head moving in quick jerks, aware like an animal sensing danger.

And then, without warning, she was on the floor writhing. Her breath had quickened. She looked so afraid. I covered her with my coat.

—Should we call an ambulance? a man asked.

—No need, I said.

I held her shaking body and, slowly, she was becalmed.

She slept all the way to Dublin and woke smiling as I led her to the ambulance. Kindly men helped her into the back of the vehicle, and she lay down. They injected her. Her eyes closed. How innocent and untroubled she looked in her sleep.

What would I tell my parents, who knew nothing of this nightmare? I pictured their bewildered faces and knew I would have to lie for another few days, until she recovered.

When we reached the hospital, I watched through the glass doors as the nurses brought her away. I took a taxi to the house of a girlfriend, and even though I drank hard and quickly, I remained sober and awake till dawn, when I headed for the early opening bar on the quays. Its curtains were closed against the morning light. The conversation was loud and at last I found blessed oblivion.

❧

Over the years, sometimes she was well. Happy in a giddy way. I thought of her as a flower in a harsh wind.

I saw the people draw away, on alert for a laugh too loud, eyes too bright, or something strange she might say to confirm her craziness. People did not trust her to be normal, talked to her like a child, and fled from her as politely as they could. Her illness brought shame and anger and awful fear. The words they use now are "schizophrenic" and "institutionalized."

At night I would dream of her in the hospital, sitting blankly in the almost bare room. Her clothes simple but their colors flattering to her dark hair and lovely face. I would see her among strangers, other patients, washing themselves over sinks. Water flowed over her hands. I would imagine her kneeling at mass, looking at the others, wondering why she was there. I could hear her sigh. The gnarled fingers of an old nun played a wheezing organ.

In the refectory, at breakfast time, I would see her eating pieces of fruit, delicately, with her fingers. Her eyes downcast, she paid no attention to the others. She was always being watched. It must have gotten on her nerves.

I could see her sitting on a bench beneath a tree, her face turned to the sunlight coming through the leaves. She never smiled in my dreams or imaginings.

Sometimes Marian would tell me about the hospital, and the pictures in my mind grew vivid. I could hear the sounds of night in the hospital. Noises in the pipes. Somewhere a woman was crying. Through her window Marian would watch the moon as it floated free, appearing and disappearing among clouds. She would try to sleep but could not. Something moved behind her eyes. Low whispers at first, faraway, then closer and closer, clearer. Voices. A cacophony of strange words, whistles and wind and discordant music. She would try to fight them off, those voices that tormented her. It would take long moments before she could control her breathing.

Then she would be up and walking fast to escape the voices, through the night corridors out into the garden. She would lie beneath the trees and find sleep.

A clock on the wall ticked the eternal time. I could see patients seated row by row in rocking chairs. They wore white masks over their eyes. The doctor placed a record on the gramophone. A piano piece, soft and echoey, filled the room. My sister rocked back and forth in her chair, giving herself over to the music. She could remember herself dancing.

Then four nurses came for her. She was restrained. She gave a violent fight and at last they got the shackles in place. A gag in her mouth, a needle in her arm. Along the corridors, woozy, lights above her blurred, and walking away she could see our father, mother, all of us disappear into the light. And there in the recess of a doorway Christ stood smiling in the shadows.

In the antiseptic coldness of the operating theater I could see Marian look with horror at the bed. Unable to move a limb, she was lifted out of the wheelchair and placed on it. Restraints again. The nurse swabbed her arm. Another needle.

—No, I heard her scream before she passed out, I don't want this.

I could see the nurse arrange a small pillow under her head, swab her temples with saline. A clamp was set between her teeth, electrodes on her temples. A switch was clicked. Her body shuddered and jerked violently as the electricity coursed through her.

I could not look at my parents' sorrowful faces, the abject way they listened to the doctor, humbling themselves before his cultured voice of authority; they were desperate for him to give some assurance that she would be well again.

—Of course, there's always hope. We should never give up hope, the doctor said.

I'll never forget the day the phone call came. I was in New York.

—Passed where? I asked foolishly.

I heard someone with an Irish accent say words softly back into my ear.

—But she's only thirty-two, I replied, as if that mattered.

And the fist tightened about my throat again, and I was thrown to the floor. Howls came out of me like a rabid dog's, until my throat was raw and I could make no more sound.

The clock on the wall ticks the seconds away. The seconds become minutes, time relentlessly moving forward, no matter what you think or wish.

I AM ALONE IN MY BROADWAY DRESSING ROOM. I have a few things around me—some good luck mementos—to remind me there is another reality. From the loudspeaker on the wall comes an announcement:

—Ladies and gentlemen of the company, this is your half-hour call. Thirty minutes to curtain.

The solitary walk from the dressing room down the stairs to the stage is a journey nobody can make for you.

Something like a stone moves in my stomach. I take up the coffee-stained script once more, but the words swim before my eyes. The huge speech in Act I. I know it backward, yet I stumble on the second paragraph and panic, cursing the syntax of Eugene O'Neill. His repetitions. Those long breathless sentences and fractured rhythms. This is one of the most difficult roles in one of his most difficult plays, *Long Day's Journey Into Night*. A portrait of a ruined man clinging to the delusion of his past, who cannot see. I've tried to find him in myself, have buried myself in the words and actions of O'Neill's creation.

The clock ticks. My breath comes shallow and fast. The stone moves again.

I began weeks ago, mumbling from the script as I moved around the rehearsal space. Self-conscious, embarrassed before my fellow actors and the director. *What are they thinking? That I'm ill-suited to this complex character, a casting mistake. Why do I find it so difficult to meet their eyes?* Uncomfortable standing or moving, my voice was high and false when I spoke. I

blushed when the director stopped me midspeech. I surrendered
to his authority hoping he would lead me to the hidden path.

Sealed off in a windowless room, I dare to take risks. To
free myself from judgment. Battle with doubt and fear of failure.
Marry movement to emotion. Be brave. Be still. Trust myself.
This Sisyphean pushing of a rock up a hill; slowly gaining confi-
dence, plunging again into confusion. I cannot escape myself yet
I know this character only in relation to myself. I must dredge
up the emotion from the well of my past.

The truth is, I don't know what acting is. Many actors have
told me the same thing. Where it comes from, why it comes to
one and not another. I've always remembered the story I was
told once by an old actor who had been in countless productions.

He said it had been a wondrous night. He had been trans-
ported to another place beyond the stage, beyond the theater
itself. He had performed the role so many times but that night
was unlike any other. His dresser came to the wings, the other
actors stared at him, understanding something marvelous was
taking place. They gazed in awe, knowing they would never see
the like of this again.

When he lifted himself from the floor at the play's end, covered in sweat and tears, to face the audience, they rose instantly
as one. There were ten curtain calls that night before he stormed
off the stage, pushing past his applauding fellow actors and stage
crew to his dressing room. He slammed the door behind him.
They could hear him shouting *fuck fuck fuck*, over and over.

Finally the dresser tapped lightly on his door and the actor
shouted for him to come in. The actor was staring into the
mirror.

—If I may be permitted to say, sir, I have never seen anything like what you did on that stage tonight. It was transcendent.

—I know, I know, said the actor.

—Then why are you so angry, sir?

—Because I have no fucking idea how I did it, he replied, his head in his hands.

I pace up and down this cage. Lie down on the floor, breathe. I find no relief. The noise of the audience begins to fill the theater like a distant sea rising and crashing.

An actor once told me he used beta-blockers to quell his performance fears. I wish I had the courage to take them, but in performance my brain operates on too many levels at once. I'm aware of the audience's words, their movement, their silence. It can feel like judgment. It might be in sympathy or not. Sudden unexpected laughter, or none at all where it was expected. Coughing, malfunctioning hearing aids, loud whispers. The constriction of my costume or shoes. Doors that won't open, missing props, random thoughts. Versions of *Did I leave the gas on?* might creep into my head in the middle of a soliloquy. How long will an audience suspend belief before they realize something is wrong? Desperately I find my way again and they are none the wiser. Mostly.

Good luck messages are pinned to the corkboard. *Break a leg, you'll be great. Thinking of you darling.* Flowers still in their plastic wrapping. I turn on John Lennon's "Beautiful Boy" and try to reach for the emotion. But nerves block that path.

I hear the sounds of the theater filling. Anticipatory chatter. The odd laugh. How many words are now in my head, waiting to spill from my brain to my mouth? What if they get stuck behind the door in my throat?

I remember the last time I was on Broadway, in another O'Neill play; we had been performing for four months, and I was emotionally and physically exhausted. In Act II, I had a huge speech that ended in my breaking down in tears. Halfway through, I noticed that someone in the front row was falling asleep, his head lolling forward. I lost my lines for an eternity of moments, then rushed and garbled my way to the end. I was furious, and as I crossed the stage for my exit, I said loudly, Wake Up!

I was determined to stand before him at the curtain call so that he would see my anger. I stared down and realized to my horror that he had a physical disability which caused his head to loll. Afterward, in my despair in the dressing room, a fellow actor said:

—You've learned a lesson tonight. The audience is never your business. Ever. Whether they are receptive or asleep or drunk, your only focus is the play.

I remembered those words when one night there was a hammering on the theater door. The knocking continued until the door was opened and a voice said:

—I have a pepperoni pizza with extra cheese, followed by a fierce whisper:

—This is a fucking theater. There's a play on. Go around the front.

My fellow actor seemed exquisitely oblivious. I only found out at our farewell party that she had been suffering from stage fright every single night of the run. She would visit her therapist before the play to get the strength to power through the performance.

Stage fright. *Dear Jesus, do not let me think about that.* I had read once that a heart monitor strapped to an actor's wrist on opening night registers the same level of stress as a passenger in a car crash. Once, I watched an actress vomit into a bucket in the wings before she entered to prolonged applause. Stephen Fry fled his dressing room and drove to Belgium from London to kill himself. God, how I understand that. Am I capable of such an action? Not to kill myself but to flee. I know I am. How long before they would notice my absence?

During rehearsals I'd been having a recurring dream of walking to the stage, having no idea of my lines, and hoping the audience would mistake my silence for meaning. Then, slowly, an awareness would spread among them that I didn't know what to say. I'd awake in a fit of anxiety and be disturbed for the day. The feeling was like a hangover.

That winter's night in Dublin, why did I not turn away from the door and head to the pub, give up all this nonsense about wanting to be an actor? A friend had said:

—You spend all your time in the picture house and the theater, why don't you join an amateur drama group?

It was advice that changed my life. In that red-tiled porch, dead flies clinging to the bulb above, I finally let the brass knocker fall, hoping it wouldn't be heard. My stomach heaved.

Stay, don't leave. Leave, don't stay. The native hue of resolution is sicklied o'er with the pale cast of thought, as Hamlet puts it. Too late. A shadow formed in the doorway.

—It's yourself, she laughed.

Who else would I be except myself? I thought.

—We've been waiting for you.

I was bid welcome by a clump of men and flush-faced women standing by the fire. Sheila, the leading actress, introduced herself. Around the dining table we read *Hamlet*, with tea and custard creams for afters. Laughter like a happy family home for Christmas. I hardly dared speak, I was timid as a hare. When it came time to read my short speech, my mouth became dry and I stammered. Everyone smiled encouragement.

Later, I walked with them to the bus stop. The girls kissed me good night, the men embraced me. Ophelia and the Ghost waved from the platform of the number eleven bus.

—Good night, sweet prince.

I realized then I had been so lonely, and this new sense of belonging overwhelmed me.

We would rehearse our avant-garde *Hamlet* in itchy polo necks with wooden swords. One Friday evening a bomb exploded streets away. Mangled bodies lay strewn in the bloodied street and for weeks afterward every car and truck in the wounded city was a potential bomb. The arrival of sectarian violence in Dublin shattered our indifference to a war only two hours away in the North of Ireland.

Yet we actors braved what might be death to reach a musty theater where we played to audiences whom we outnumbered. Many nights there was no audience at all, but I knew nothing would stop me from this way of life. I was so proud to be an amateur actor playing a role with only a few lines in a Shakespeare play.

And there were the players. George, an insurance company manager, a Laurence Olivier manqué with a fake fur coat and booming voice, taught me to breathe from the diaphragm when I'd gulp and swallow my words.

—I've played Vanya, Iago, Lear. If I'd gone professional, I doubt if I'd ever have played those great parts. Insurance is my job, acting is my passion, he would declare.

We toured the country in a rented laundry van. Sometimes we stayed overnight in bed-and-breakfasts at drama festivals. Crushes consummated in creaking beds. I loved the gossip in pubs after a show.

—The Queen is slipping it to Horatio, and the second gravedigger.

—And the geck of her, as if butter wouldn't melt.

—How his nibs got cast as the cripple in that last play is beyond me!

—Sure he didn't even know which leg he was supposed to be limping on half the time.

—Hamlet, my arse.

—So listen, said the Queen, I'm doing my big speech and I declare to God, the audience starts to laugh because that eejit who's supposed to be dead is lying there breathing in and out like he's just run a four-minute mile. I was as pleasant as I could be afterward. Young man, I says, you need to study breath control. And he just stands there looking at me, with the mouth hanging open like a skipping rope. Not to mention the mumbling.

—Oh the mumbling, don't get me going, dear. Sometimes I despair of this younger generation of actors. No value on training and technique.

—That Marlon Brando has a lot to answer for, said King Claudius.

⟨∂⟩∞⟨∂⟩

I decided I would try to become a full-time actor and so I joined the extras' union.

My first appearance before a camera was as an extra in a program about a new club for transvestites which had opened in Dublin city center. The director placed me at the bar to make the place look less bare and so I made my television debut as Drinker Number Four, in my leather jacket, with my back to the camera. Afterward we all got drunk, high heels kicked off, skirts hiked, bracelets rattling.

In that same leather jacket months later I entered Madigan's Pub. Wesley Burrowes, the writer of a national soap opera set in a farming community called *The Riordans*, noticed me and asked if I'd like to audition for a major role he was writing. I was cast as a kind of Irish Heathcliff. The program had already been running for seventeen years, at a time when Ireland was a one-channel land and the country came to a standstill for the show.

I'd been having some success in the theater but this exposed me immediately to a national audience. A magazine contacted me and wanted to do a feature to be tentatively titled "At Home with a Rising Star." They wanted to photograph me relaxing away from the glamor of the set. At the time I was living in a one-bedroom flat in a dodgy part of the city. When they saw where I lived, no lock on my door, drug addicts and dealers in the hallways, and a man upstairs who sold fake handbags, and after a friend told them it was the only flat in Dublin you had to wipe your feet on the way out of, the journalist recommended an alternative location for what he called the shoot.

In a show flat, in a striped apron, surrounded by pots and pans and utensils I'd obviously never used, never mind seen before, I smiled stiffly for the photographer who repeated, *Great. Great.* Did he not see the cold sore that was erupting on my lip which I'd tried to cover with Vaseline and a little talcum powder?

—Down the lens over your shoulder. That's the ticket. Great, great.

After the shoot, the writer interviewed me about my new life. Did I have a girlfriend? What did I like to do in my spare time? What were my favorite bands, singers, colors? I'd never been asked those questions by anybody ever. In fact, nobody had shown much interest in what I had to say about anything.

What did I feel about being a sex symbol? I was mortified by this question. I'd never thought of myself as handsome, the opposite in fact, with my thrice-broken nose and beetroot-colored face, webbed with broken veins. I was socially awkward and anxious except when I drank and then I couldn't be shut up. My nails were bitten to the quick, my clothes putrid from cigarette smoke, my eyes someone had described as two mournful piss holes in the snow.

Once when I was stoned, I watched *The Hunchback of Notre Dame* with Charles Laughton, and I thought I could identify with him. I had enormous self-esteem issues, though I didn't know the name of the condition then. I often felt worthless, untalented, fearful of criticism, and suspicious of praise. Yet now strangers were shoveling praise on me and asking for my autograph. A woman in a bar whipped off her bra and asked me to sign it. Schoolgirls chased me in the street.

Weeks later, I was walking down the Rathmines Road when I saw myself grinning on the cover of a magazine, wearing the striped apron and holding a brand-new saucepan.

I watched my first episode with my family. It was my parents' favorite show at the time. There was silence. Then I appeared lugging a bale of hay.

—Jesus, my sister said.

Even during the commercials none of us knew what to say. When it was over my father spoke.

—Isn't television a wonderful thing? There you are, he said, pointing at the television, and there you are, he said, pointing to me in the chair.

One of the perks of being on the telly was that we got invited to open supermarkets, judge beauty competitions, and the like. One of the other actors advised me to invest in a white suit for these occasions, to add a touch of glamor.

—The punters expect a bit of glitz, he assured me.

I received an offer to lead a walk for a youth center in a country town and was being paid five hundred pounds for the day, cash in hand, plus, of course, all the drink I could consume. When I reached the village, there was no sign of life in the empty streets and I thought I had the day wrong. It was like that town in *High Noon* just before Gary Cooper goes out to confront the bad guy. But it was because everyone was in the football field at the end of the town, which was jammed with old and young all gathered to see the famous actor from the television. I stepped out of the car in my white bell-bottomed suit and Cuban heels into a frenzy of

backslapping and hand grabbing and wonder at this weird creature they knew only from television come to life before them.

One of the local councilors, dressed as a jarvey and holding
a whip, introduced himself.

—You look just like yourself, he told me as he led me to a
waiting pony and trap into which I was hooshed by the crowd.
We came to a raised platform, upon which sat a local politician
decked out in his party's colors and beside him, of course, the
inevitable parish priest, an elderly bewildered man with a glass
eye. There was a screech of feedback from the microphone—
furthermore . . . great honor . . . all the way . . . further ado—and
at the announcement of my name a cheer erupted. I embraced a
fake-tanned girl around whose neck I placed the ribbon for win-
ner of the local beauty competition.

—Go on, ya biy ya, put that girl down, you don't know
where she's been, someone shouted from the crowd to big laughter, the hecklers silenced by the one-eyed glare of the old priest.

I was in the middle of a speech about how honored I was
to be there when umbrellas opened.

—Let's get on with the walk before the heavens open on us,
said the politician. We went out onto the road, me at the helm
like the pied piper while behind marched the band, all drums and
brass and cymbals. Soon the drizzle had become a shower and
we were forced to take shelter beneath trees.

—I don't like the looka that sky.

—Who'd ever have thought I'd be sheltering under a tree
with yourself?

—Would you leave the man be!

—What's it like being an actor? How do youse remember
all them words? You must have a quare memory.

—Is it real drink youse do be drinkin?

—You're not the first big name we've had here.

—We met Jayne Mansfield herself.

—Sure she was only going to the toilet in Kelly's pub beyont on her way to Tralee.

—It was just before she got killed in that accident in England.

—Big fur coat on her and a little dog she had.

—Taking photos and signing autographs, not a bother on her.

With only another five miles to go we trudged on, but then the skies opened in earnest and we all repaired to the pub. I bought a round for everyone. A singsong started up.

Several hours later I stumbled into the street and found no trace of the driver who was to return me in my sodden white suit to the city.

A timid adolescent approached. He asked me about the life of an actor, and did I have to study for a long time. He was dreaming of becoming an actor too and wanted to know how I knew I was one. I told him that years ago I saw the traveling players perform in the seminary, and I just knew watching them that's what I wanted to be.

—Follow your heart. If acting is what you want to do, nothing will stop you, I said.

He told me that he had cycled the seven miles there and back to his house just to meet me. I look back at that kid and think he could have been me.

❦

By 1992, I was starting to make a name in Hollywood. *The Usual Suspects* was still a few years away and the big movie that year was *Dracula*, to be directed by Francis Ford Coppola.

I had lunch with my agent in Beverly Hills. He was obsessed with food, studied the menu intently while holding a pen with a small light on its tip.

—That brandy and cream pasta looks delicious, he said.

The waiter congratulated him on his choice, as if he had just spelled a very hard word.

—Can I have it without the sauce? he asked. Could you make it a starter portion?

Absolutely he could.

—Why don't you just get them to take a photograph and put it on the plate? I said.

My agent had a huge office. All its windows looked out over the city. On his desk were photographs of dogs; on the walls, signed photographs of his extremely famous clients, including leading politicians of the Republican Party, with American flags behind them.

He had several phones and worked them using a headset that made him look like a pilot talking to air traffic control. It allowed him to move about the office, mouthing instructions to his assistant as he engaged producers, casting agents, directors. When he spoke, it was with charming authority. He was fiercely loyal but always on the hunt for new star clients even if he had previously disparaged them. He had taken several clients from obscurity to world fame.

He earned millions of dollars per year and received huge bonuses. He was ruthless in negotiations, slamming down the phone on studios:

—Call us when you get real with the offer. I won't insult my client by bringing that to him.

He would spend his weekends reading scripts at his beach house.

—*Dracula* has everything, he said, seduction, insanity, decapitation, rape, demons. It won't be a conventional interpretation. Francis has created images based on Cocteau's *Beauty and the Beast* and the Japanese Noh tradition. No computer-generated trickery. He will be using hand-cranked cameras and techniques from early films.

Every actor in Hollywood wanted to audition.

I had been lucky in that since making *Miller's Crossing* in 1990, I'd been sent scripts and no longer had to audition. Auditioning was an appalling process that I found difficult and often embarrassing. The memory of an experience at the Royal Shakespeare Company in which I used a motorcycle helmet as the skull of Yorick still haunted me.

Once, I had to pretend to be hanging off a cliff with one hand as a torrential river raged below. I was splayed out on the floor, breathless and perspiring. I was supposed to be holding another climber with my free hand. After much grunting and groaning I hauled my imaginary partner to safety on top of the cliff.

I stood breathless before the producer and director, who riffled through their pages.

—I think you forgot some dialogue there.

—Yes, you did, there's a line to your friend.

—It's "Hang on, Tim."

—That's kind of implied, isn't it? I said. He's hanging off the cliff so it seems kind of obvious that that's all he can do.

—That's what's scripted here.

So I did it again on the bare floor, this time with the dialogue.

—Can you shout? There's a wind blowing and Tim will need to hear you. He will never hear you at that level.

So now I was shouting against an imagined wind, snow, and thunder.

—That's great. And cut. Just one thing, the director said, if you don't mind. You're nailing this but would you mind trying it in American English? What we're going for is a kind of mid-Atlantic vibe.

So down again I went at it with the full mid-Atlantic.

—Great to meet you, said the producer as he bounced a baseball in a leather mitten. The director only nodded because he was so famous.

I hated auditions.

—Look, I know you hate the process of auditioning, but Coppola is insisting on everyone doing it. And I know how you hate dressing for the part but this time, trust me, you need to.

—But Dracula is a vampire, I said.

—You've got to suggest darkness, seduction, mystery. He's a sexy character.

—Have you ever seen *Nosferatu*? Klaus Kinski has pointy bat ears and one tooth, and he's as bald as an egg, I said.

—I'm thinking more Frank Langella, he said. I know Francis is going to be so impressed that you took the time to think the character through. And you'll be the only one.

I wasn't so sure about that, all those method types sleeping in coffins to get into character.

At the studio gate the security man looked at my slicked-back hair, my black suit and black shirt.

—Building on your left.

An assistant crossed my name off the list.

—Anything I can get you: Coke, water, coffee, tea?

I pushed open the door and before me were twelve Draculas, all with slicked-back hair and dark suits. Every well-known actor in Hollywood held in his hand the same three pages.

⁂

Shortly after the audition, I was invited to an industry dinner party. The conversation drifted to matters spiritual. The guests were talking about the charisma of a master they knew, a holy man in touch with the soul. He believed that through diet, prayer, and a certain amount of self-discipline based on Celtic spiritual practices we could transcend our human frailty.

Cold mushroom juice was passed around, a disgusting concoction. It reminded me of a laxative my mother made for us from senna pods, back when parents believed children's health depended on being flushed out at least once a week. I was seated next to a plant so was able to dispose of it discreetly.

The guests were singers and actors mostly. To my right was a heavily bejeweled woman with a pale face and dark hair. We exchanged some pleasantries about the earthquake and living in Los Angeles versus New York. Weirdly she was fascinated by Irish fishermen in Aran sweaters.

—They are sooo hot.

A large man arrived in a kimono just covering his sandals. His feet had a bluish hue, indicating bad circulation. He received deference. *Did he really have the answer to life?* I wondered. If so, why he was sporting a ridiculous bouffant hairstyle. He was placed at the top of the table and began to pontificate on the pagan world. I took my leave.

I became aware of the clack of high heels behind me. It was the bejeweled woman. She offered to drive me to my car, which was only a few streets away.

—Nobody in Los Angeles walks, she said.

I got in. Her black Mercedes purred like a cat. She hit a button and music filled the car.

—Recognize that? she asked. It's the soundtrack to your movie *Defense of the Realm*. Pachelbel's Canon.

Finally, we reached my car.

—Sure you don't want a ride home? she asked.

—No, I'm fine, I replied. We bid each other good night.

I pulled onto Sunset Boulevard. A mile or so on, I glanced in the mirror. She was behind me. *She's probably taking it easy, driving carefully*, I reasoned. I forgot about her until I looked in the mirror again. *Could she be following me?*

I sped up. She did too.

I cut down to Beverly Drive. She was still behind me.

I headed back to Sunset Boulevard. There was hardly any traffic. Still, she was there, maintaining her speed and distance.

At San Vicente, the lights were against me. She drew up alongside my car, smiled and waved, and then took off before me at speed.

I pulled up at my house in Beverley Hills. I was about to put the key in the door when I heard her car.

—Lovely to meet you, she said, as her window ascended with a slow whine and she was encased again in blackness. Then she was gone.

I turned on all the lights in the house to rid myself of the unnerving feeling that I was still being watched.

One morning several days later I noticed a woman sitting on the wall of the house opposite. It was the woman from the party. And she was knitting an Aran sweater from a ball of white wool, her red hair now styled in a bob. I went outside and approached her cautiously.

—What are you doing here? I asked.

—Oh hi, she said. I know your size, she continued as the needles clicked.

—What are you doing here? I asked again.

—Being near you inspires me, she said.

Weeks passed. I forgot the strange encounter and then one morning, opening the window, I noticed little envelopes attached to the stems of flowers in my garden. In each, sealed with a kiss, was a line of poetry.

I was uneasy for days, feeling invaded and vulnerable. But for months there was nothing until one night I answered the phone and it was her voice.

—Hello, darling, I just had to call.

—How did you get my number?

She giggled.

—I'm a girl who knows how to find out things.

I began to feel scared. I flipped back the curtain and saw the street was empty. There was a gentle knocking at the door. I thought about the scene in *Wuthering Heights* where Lockwood is woken by a branch tapping against the window. A shiver ran through my body. I was scaring myself. *Pull it together.*

There was no one at the door when I opened it. I left my house and walked slowly down the path. I turned toward the house, and there she stood in the doorway.

—Baby, don't hang up on me like that again, please don't. Let's tell each other that we're sorry.

I was sure she had a gun and that I would be shot dead in my own driveway.

I moved toward her, took her by the arm, and pulled her away. Then I went in and closed the door.

Days later, the phone rang and clicked to the answering machine and her sweet, reasonable tones:

—Baby, let's work this out, I love you so much, you mean the world to me. I only want what's good for us.

The police were powerless because I couldn't prove anything.

—Guess it comes with the territory, one of them said and shrugged.

NOW HERE I AM ON BROADWAY. Opening night. And there you are, Mother, sitting in the corner, handbag on your lap. The Theatre Royal was where you took us mostly, where Judy Garland sang from the window of her dressing room to the crowds below in the alleyway, where Roy Rogers and his wife Dale performed, and Trigger his Wonder Horse reared up and neighed to the music onstage. We were amazed they had come from way out in the Wild West of America, and now here they were in Dublin, talking and singing right in front of us. We went mental with excitement when Roy drew his six-guns and twirled them, then lassoed a boy in the front row. Later, someone cut some hairs off Trigger's tail and sold them for souvenirs.

Every weekend, the curtain with "safety" written across it would rise to reveal a different backdrop. Beneath the stage, the band played. "There's No Business Like Show Business!" Adults lit cigarettes and passed sweets to children, who strained on the edges of their seats. A man in a white jacket trotted onto the stage, red carnation in his lapel. He pointed to the band and we all clapped like mad things. Irish dancers with pipe-cleaner legs in silver-buckled shoes clattered across the floor, ringlets tossing. The audience kept time with their feet. A glittering, smiling woman flew on a trapeze back and forth past the moon. A man with a handlebar mustache pretended to be a bird whistling to music. A magician asked for a volunteer and a boy ran up to be placed in a box and abracadabra-ed away. He appeared again at the back of the theater, flushed with fame and safe after all, to wild cheers from the audience.

Best of all, we children loved the ventriloquist, in a checked suit, who had a dummy called Finnegan, with red cheeks and a monocle over his swiveling eye. We felt like Finnegan represented us, and we cheered for his rebellious cursing at the adults onstage.

—I hope you're going to behave yourself tonight, Finnegan, I don't want to hear any bad language from you in front of all these good children.

—Bloody Hell, said Finnegan, and his head turned toward us as we howled with laughter.

—Now I'm warning you, Finnegan. You promised you'd be good.

—No I bloody didn't.

—That's it, I'm going to have to put you in the trunk.

—No! we roared in solidarity with our little wooden hero.

—I was right to put him in the box, wasn't I, boys and girls? Finnegan will you promise to be a good boy if I let you out?

From inside the box came the sound of Finnegan pleading.

—Let me out, I'll be good.

His head appeared slowly.

—I'm sorry, Finnegan, for locking you in the box.

—You can go feck off with yourself.

The curtain would fall on the two of them wrestling as the band struck up a finale to the sound of our howls of joy.

Later the people poured out into the street humming the music or repeating the comedian's jokes, laughing all over again.

When we were older, you would take us to the Abbey Theatre. The people who went to the Abbey were different to those who went to the Royal. They spoke like they came from rich parts of the city. The men wore suits and the women fur coats. They fanned themselves with programs and shared boxes of After Eight mint chocolates with each other.

I loved the colors of the costumes, the lights, the painted backdrops, the way the actors were more like real people than real people. The plays were like dreams that were real. And when the actors bowed at the end, they seemed different, as if they had become themselves again. As if they had removed masks. It was more enchanting to watch than snow falling on Christmas Day. You gave me my lifelong love of the theater.

Why did I choose this life? The life of an actor. Destiny was it? Maybe the signs had been there all along. I had been surrounded in real life by actors in the theater of the street. I was an observer of the characters of my childhood. I would imagine them being actors in my own made-up plays. Like the traveling storyteller, who knew about timing: the pause, the whisper, the slowing down and speeding up of words. Who knew how to sprinkle humor and tension. Who made us believe in giants, in death becoming the wind, and the god Balor, who could turn the reeds of the lake red with the fury of his one mad eye. But soon, the flickering blue-and-white glass of television replaced him.

Like the strongman who lived in a tent by the roadside. He was a fierce silent man who seemed to need no company. But at weekends we'd see him down by the bridge, surrounded by crowds, his dogs guarding the hat he passed around to collect money. A volunteer would strap him into a straightjacket, fasten the thick straps as he stood as if in a trance. Within minutes he would have broken free, to the amazement of the crowd. He neither smiled nor acknowledged them. He chewed nails and swallowed them. He lay on broken glass, grinding the shards into his bare back. I wanted to learn those tricks so that I could go around the roads of Ireland myself. I wondered what power he had, to make people silent with awe. It was the same power

I would eventually witness in the great actors I would come to work with.

Or like Titus the liar. Titus swore black was white and up was down; you couldn't believe the day of the week out of his mouth.

—Here lads, did I ever tell yiz the time I took over the control of a jet after the pilot had a heart attack? Landed her neat as a bird on a bush. Well, the round of applause they gave me!

Once he put Tanfastic on his face and said he'd been in Spain, though everyone knew he was at his sister's place in Kilcock because his fingers were orange but his palms were white.

—O lads, it's some place, Spain. Sure don't talk to me, they know how to enjoy life over there. There's some as don't take to the heat, but not yours truly. Not a bother on me. Out all hours, even when the natives can't hack it.

Here, did I tell yiz I ate a curry once that was so hot, not even the Indians could look at it. Finished it and asked for more, never seen the likes of it, they said.

Here, did yiz know Hitler didn't top himself. Not at all! Escaped out of Germany, and do yiz know where he landed up? In Dublin. Has a fish-and-chip shop off of Capel Street. Large-as-life mustache and all, serving out fish and chips, not a bother on him.

Did I ever tell yiz I slept in a coffin for a week in a haunted house? Had an awful job to wake me up in the morning, I was that sound asleep.

Here, did I ever tell yiz about the time I was out in the Congo beyont in Africa, and a gansey-load of Baloobas came at me, fierce mad crowd altogether. Put you in a pot and eat you without salt, they would.

"Leave down them spears," sez I. They didn't know what to make of Titus at all.

"Don't have me to say it again," sez I, very severe like. "Put down them spears on the ground where I can see them." And like little childer they did as they were told, got such a fright with the roars of me.

And here lads, did I ever tell yiz about the time I saw the king of Hell, Lucifer himself? True fact. Where? says you! Above on that hill where the old ruin is, is where!

I knocked on the door one night and I stuck for somewhere to bed down. Next thing, the door is opened by this fella in a black cloak, and didn't he grab me by the collar and pull me inside and throw me into a heap on the floor. Next thing, what came into the room but a huge black cat with two bendy horns instead of ears and burning coals instead of eyes, and the place filled up with the smell of sulfur and smoke and the cat hopped up onto a kind of throne and all these other divils filed in and started to toast him.

"All hail king of the dark," says they.

I'll admit the heart went crossways in me and I made a run for it, with all the divils after me, across the hill like the clappers till I got home. When I woke up, I thought it was a dream I was after having till I looked in the mirror, and wasn't me face covered in scratch marks where the cat had scrawbed at me. Not a word of a lie, lads.

Here lads, did I ever tell yiz . . .

And there was the sad-eyed traveler woman, with her baby wrapped in a shawl.

—God bless you, missus, and a long life to you.

My mother brought her in for a mug of tea and a sandwich.

—The blessings of God on you, missus, you're a good woman. There's some as would shut the door in your face and run you.

Words spilled out of her.

—I always had the tinkers' blood in me even though I was from a settled family, always knew it.

Where did I meet me man himself, you say, missus? At the horse fair in Ballinasloe, where else? Smelling of smoke and milk, and the scar along the side of his mouth gave him a kind of sneer. Asked me as bold as brass if I'd like a ride in his trap, but I wasn't afraid of him. More like he was of me. And he, standing there, holding the little door open with its brass clasp, clicking his tongue and giving his rough commands to the jennet, cracking the whip on her bony back, his legs apart showing himself off, eyes boring into me like a drill, heating up the blood in me, his hand with the tattoo and the silver rings lightly holding the reins.

And didn't my mother in the garden see us as we galloped past our house, between the hedges, and she let out a scream and me father came running, shouting, but the tinker paid no heed and didn't me dress lift up and I pushed it down and held it, my hair whipping my face out past Doyle's field and Doran's Cross, the jennet's ears straight up and then sudden as you like, "Whoa," says he, pulling against the wind, and we come to a halt and he lets me down in the road and without "By your leave" takes off again with never a backward glance. It was only his way of trying to win me but he needn't have, sure don't you know, missus, I'd have gone anywhere with him.

⌒⍬⌒

I begin to apply my makeup. My mask. Our tragedy, O'Neill said, is that we are haunted not just by the masks others wear but by the masks we wear ourselves. We all act all the time. Life makes us necessary deceivers. Except maybe when we are alone. As I am now in the windowless dressing room of a Broadway theater.

I struggle with authenticity. Being truthful. Both to myself first and to other people. Is it possible to be completely honest with myself? To admit my fears, my demons, prejudices, the petty envies, the unfulfilled desires? I want to live an authentic life. To take off the mask requires courage. I admit my fragility, my vulnerability and weakness. Why are we so afraid to let others see us as we truly are ? Can you ever really know another human being? There is a locked room which we ourselves dare not enter for fear. Fear of what exactly I don't know. Maybe that is one of the necessities of fiction. It allows us to experience the hidden depths of ourselves and to acknowledge that we are all made of the same human stuff.

I am by nature an introvert. For a long time I was ashamed of this. As if it were somehow a moral failing. I never felt I belonged anywhere. Was always trying to be as real as I could. Seeking authenticity. But paralyzed by my mask and the masks of others. I can be sociable too. But it drains me of energy and I have to find refuge in solitude again. I have few friends. That also used to mortify me. Aren't you supposed to have huge parties where scores of successful witty people surround you?

No one else can play the part of me.

—You can't trust actors, a producer said to me once, half-jokingly, because they are always pretending. They lie.

—No, I replied, our job is to try to tell the truth. We are the channels through which the truth comes. There is no play without the actor, no actor without the words.

I look into the mirror. My father's face looks back at me. I see him dipping his cut-throat in the rainwater barrel, shaving in the cracked mirror which divides his face in two.

—Do you remember the time I finally got you to come for a meal in a restaurant?

—Sure where would I be going eating a meal in a restaurant and having to pay through the nose for food you could get in the supermarket for a quarter of the price?

—That's not the point. I wanted to treat you.

—Sure treat me for what?

—Just. That's all.

You were dressed in your one good suit, collar and tie under the pullover. Shoes, as always, polished. Your only extravagance.

—You can tell a man by his shoes, you always said.

We were shown to our table by a deferential waiter. He made a big show of saying he was a fan. He ignored you until I introduced you.

—A pleasure to meet you, sir, he said, bowing slightly from the waist.

—Jaysus, these are huge menus. You'd have to pass an exam just to read them. You wouldn't know what half of these yokes are.

At home I rarely saw you sit at the table. There was never enough room in the kitchen for us all to sit together so you would stand with one hand leaning on the chair and bless yourself before and after each meal.

The waiter brought a selection of breads. Whole wheat, peasant raisin, sourdough rye, pumpkin.

—I'd like a bit of brown, if you have it, you said. You always loved Mother's brown bread.

—If I may recommend our lobster bisque, offered the waiter.

You used to make soup from the boiled heads of sheep and pigs, and chew the pig's ears and feet, with fried bread and dripping.

—There's great nourishment in the brains too, you'd say. You used to cook huge pots of rice and a lumpy thing called sago.

—You're not cooking for soldiers in a barracks, Mother would say.

—Did you know that in the Siege of Drogheda the people were that hungry they had to eat rats? An awful bastard Cromwell. The curse of God on him.

—Please, Dad, not now.

—Have you had a chance to look at the wine list, gentlemen?

—Would they give me a pint of Guinness, do you think? you whispered to me.

—They'll get you anything you want.

—You don't have to be spending all this money. You have to look after your pennies and the pounds will take care of themselves, a wise man said. You were always quoting this wise man, whoever he was.

We were uneasy together in the formality of the restaurant. Halfway into your pint you became expansive.

—You did well for yourself getting your degree at the university. The first of the family ever to get to a university. And a scholarship no less. And now you're on the television. You're as well known as Doran's donkey.

—Remember when I asked you to come and see me in my first play? And you asked how much it was to get in? I told you five quid and you said, Sure I can see you at home for nothing.

—You were bollock naked in it.

—Only for a few seconds.

—Nearly had to cart your mother off to intensive care. I thought you would have stuck at the old plumbing game.

—I wasn't cut out for it. I was useless.

—Still you can't beat a trade, as the fella says. It'll always stand to you.

You ordered another pint and the food arrived.

You said to the waiter:
—Them spuds are tasty alright, grand bit of meat too.
There was more silence. We made small talk about the restaurant. Football. You lit your pipe. The bill arrived.
—What's the damage? you asked.
—Doesn't matter. It's my treat.
—Sure let me go halves.
—No.
—Go on. Tell us how much.
—Seventeen pounds, if you must know.
—Seventeen pounds. Lord Jaysus. At least Dick Turpin had the courtesy to wear a mask when he robbed people.

Every morning, my father and his friends would walk three miles to the chapel for early mass and then into the taproom of the Guinness brewery, a pint of undiluted stout to start the day. They were coopers' laborers, hauling and shaving and planing wood for the staved barrels that would be rolled to the trucks and ferried off to the docks for England, or to the barges to bring porter to the faraway towns of Ireland. My father was proud of that ancient trade and the language that went with it.

Then, one day, they were told they would be needed no more. That they were laborers, not skilled men. On the scrap heap at forty-eight years of age, too young to retire, too old to find another job in a changing world. They got a lump sum, a small pension, and a clock. After thirty years.

—What use is a fucking clock only to remind you of how fast the years have gone and the few you've got left?

There was a dinner to which all the families were invited. Speeches were made by managers they rarely met. Applause and toasts and photographs.

To be on the scrap heap was to be shamed. A man worked, he brought home wages in a brown packet, placed them on the mantelpiece, and was handed back a few pounds by his wife for cigarettes and beer. But there was no talk of feelings or emotional pain, so my father sought refuge in silence.

He got a part-time job trimming hedges, and even though it was odd-job work, he put on a tie because he was going to work for a posh woman who he said was gentry. She didn't like "the laborers," as she called them, to eat in the house. I would think of my father sitting looking at her big house as he ate his sandwiches in the garden. Then winter came and there was no need for him anymore, and he wasn't called back in spring or summer. Our mother became the breadwinner, working in the hospital, the one who left early now and didn't return until late.

Every day, my father would take the dog for a walk on the hill road. Later when he got sick, I took over walking her. She would skid to a halt outside the pub and go straight to the barman.

—That dog would sit up on the stool and order himself a pint and a bag of crisps, the barman laughed.

After that job as a gardener, my father never worked again. But still he kept that cheap clock on the shelf, winding it every night, though it was always ticking too slow or too fast.

His wavy hair that all the women admired turned thin and grey. He became stooped and walked with labored breath, his clothes loose about his body, specks of dried blood where the razor grazed him; his hands had begun to shake, and he seemed bewildered by life.

He had never questioned the political and economic system which condemned him to the scrap heap.

—You live the life you are given, he always said.

For the 2017 Academy Awards, Rolex wanted to acknowledge actors who had worn their watches in film. There was Paul Newman, Marlon Brando, Peter Sellers, Benicio del Toro, Charles

Bronson, and myself, among a few others. I received a gold time-piece with my name inscribed on the back, a one-off special edi-tion. Paul Newman's 1968 Rolex Daytona sold at auction for fifteen million dollars after twelve minutes to a bidder on the telephone, the highest price ever paid for a wristwatch.

—A world gone mad, I could hear you say. The biggest sin is wasting time. When your ship comes in, make sure you're on the dock to meet it, as the wise man said.

It's funny how I half-listened to you, or didn't listen at all, for so many years. It's only now I hear you.

When you died at the hospital, they brought us what they called your "effects": toothbrush, razor, prayer book, the clothes you thought you would go home in; all that remained of you. The most valuable thing you owned, a vintage watch from the fifties with a cream dial, the numbers picked out in gold, Swiss made, seventeen jewels in a stainless steel case, water-resistant and antimagnetic. The brown band frayed with your sweat. It had been on your wrist as long as I could remember, beneath the crooked tattoo of a crucifix.

—You have to wind this fella with care between your finger and thumb, always in a forward direction.

As you got older you would bring it closer to your eyes, squint at it as I made to go, anxious to be away.

Later, when I'd visit you, you'd say:

—You can stay a few minutes yet. I'll put the kettle on.

Now I understand that was your way of telling me you loved me. Hanging onto those last moments between us.

Late one night on the Bridge of Sighs in Venice, as I strag-gled back to my hotel after a night of drinking, I was pointing down to the canal when your watch slipped from my wrist into its dark depths. Maybe jewelry comes into one's life for a rea-son and leaves for a reason, and like everything in this world we must be prepared to let it go. Yet so many times I have imagined the journey of your watch to the silt below, imagined it resting there, not rusted but shining, still ticking, real as anything and forever unreachable. Like the past.

⟬◦⟭

I move closer to the mirror with my eyebrow pencil and trace a line, delicately.

—Not too heavy now. You don't want to look like Groucho Marx. Next, the brush to take down the red. Don't go too pale though—it'll wash you out under the lights.

Once I was looking in the hall mirror of the school. The brother smacked me in the side of the head.

—That's all you're any good for! Admiring yourself and thinking about girls.

I was not admiring myself or thinking of girls. I was looking at myself, at the face of a strange boy who might not be real, a ghost perhaps, inside the glass.

He followed me all my life. I would see his shivering face in river water, whenever I passed a shop window, this face of the boy who was me and not me. The mirror is everywhere, sees everything, remembers everything. The priest's face trembling in the golden chalice at mass. My mother opening a makeup shell to look at herself. Our neighbor Mr. Cullen, black caterpillar eyebrows, staring at me in the back seat through his rearview mirror, smiling tombstone teeth when he took us children on a Sunday drive in the mountains. The priest in the sacristy before the mass seemed an ordinary man, touching his hair in the mirror, staring into it for long moments mumbling words to himself.

The set for *In Treatment*, a series I did for HBO, was at the Paramount Studios where *The Lucy Show* had been filmed. I was working fourteen-hour days playing a therapist. It was always just me and one other actor, the patient. Cooped up in the studio with no air doing take after take, I would long for my hour lunch break.

Many days, I would walk to the nearby Hollywood Forever Cemetery, the graveyard of the great Hollywood stars. The Forever Cemetery is more of a theme park than a cemetery, a place where you can contemplate life and death, as well as the ephemeral nature of fame. *Sic transit gloria mundi*, it says on more than one headstone. The cemetery was segregated until 1959. Hattie McDaniel, who won an Oscar for her role in *Gone with the Wind*, was refused a plot there because she was Black.

Rudolph Valentino's is still the most visited grave there. Known as the Latin Lover, he changed the way the world thought about sex and seduction, though he came to despise his brooding lover image. He was blamed for America's supposed descent into homosexual degeneracy. There were charges that he was in a "lavender marriage." When he died, a hundred thousand hysterical women wept and several committed suicide.

From the cemetery you can see the Hollywood sign, the promise that your dreams can come true. But in 1932, Peg Entwistle's dream did not materialize for her, as it doesn't for so many. One day, she walked up the canyon, climbed one-hundred feet to the sign, and threw herself off. She was twenty-four years old. The sad irony is that the day after she jumped, she was going to be offered a leading role in a play.

On one of my walks, I came upon a ceremony. People were standing in a tent, laughing and talking as champagne was being poured. A woman, in her eighties perhaps, spoke into a microphone, welcoming her guests to the celebration. It was a death party.

—I want to give thanks for my life while I am still around, she said. Everyone applauded. I've had a most marvelous time here. I've been given great gifts. There has been tragedy too. My beloved husband and my child. My diagnosis is terminal, as you all know, so I want to celebrate my death, as I have lived my life. With joy and gratitude. And I want to celebrate with you, all my dearest ones.

She had commissioned a documentary with clips of her friends and children talking about her.

A tassel hung from a silken drape that covered a structure next to the tent. When the film ended, she pulled on the tassel to reveal a mausoleum that she had designed herself. Everyone applauded again.

—Anytime you feel like coming to visit, she said, you can see the video of my life here on earth by pressing the button on the console.

The Forever Cemetery reminded me of our local undertaker in Dublin, Pat, who brought succor to the bereaved in low whispers in his Sunday-suited best, his face a mask of professional sympathy. All those who once breathed upon the earth, he knew their stories.

Pat would say:

—The name, the year of birth, the year of death, and the small dash in between. That dash is all the days of your life. The graveyard is the only true democracy. No winners here, no losers. It is the garden of the dead. I'm the last to touch the body before it goes to its maker. For that reason I will always have the utmost respect for the dignity of the dead person. If they leave suddenly, there might be an energy trapped and you'd wait till that drifted away, but you can never really know when the soul departs. You have to remember you are in the presence of the eternal.

I've seen everything—fistfights and fucking in the bushes and a fellow once who couldn't stop laughing at his wife's funeral or the drunkard who fell into a grave and pulled in another eejit with him. Your daddy would recall a couple who came back from England, a child of six or seven they had, though they weren't married. There was talk, of course, of them living in sin outside the sacrament of marriage and all that class of carry-on. By the by, the man fell sick, and he got sicker and sicker till he was just a bag of bones, and he wasn't seen for months, unable to leave the house. We all knew the end was near and sure enough one night the woman came to the door here, in an awful way. I washed the poor man and laid him out in his Sunday suit on the kitchen table, and I sent her to call the priest down with the solicitor and the doctor. We pulled the curtains closed against the neighbors. We knew what it was we had to do. She came from the bedroom arrayed in her bridal gown down the stairs and stood beside the corpse. On his finger, she placed a wedding ring, and there before the solicitor and myself as witness the priest sanctified the marriage of the dead man to the woman.

If you ask me, there's too much rush now to put the person into the ground. Not like in the days of the old people when they'd hold wakes and there would be drinking and eating, singing and stories told while the body of the deceased lay among them. They would look on the face of death itself and be reminded of the gift of life.

My father used to joke when I was young that he wanted to be buried in Sutton:

—The best view of any graveyard in Ireland.

But there are just bones down there, and skulls; unless you were a saint and your body didn't rot like ordinary people's.

—All your own, going back generations, is buried there. May they and all the souls of the faithful departed rest in peace. And when your time comes, make sure it is among them, and not off in some place where no one knows your story.

I think of a moment I witnessed at the Deauville Film Festival in 2003. A famous actress, in mink and perfume, with an ancient mask of a face, stood before the lift.

—Please wait, she ordered the attendant in an English accent as her jeweled fingers stayed the elevator gate. An old man came along the corridor, step by tiny step, hand outstretched toward her, anxiously gripping her arm tightly.

—I'm here, darling, she said tenderly. Don't worry. I'm not going anywhere without you.

—I thought I'd lost you, he said, in a voice of phlegm. She touched his hand as we descended. The man's labored breathing filled the silence.

The lift stopped, and the attendant held the gates open for them. They clung tight to one another as they moved across the foyer like frightened children in the dark.

As ye are now so soon shall we be—the phrase comes unbidden to my mind. It was one of your sayings, Mother.

In the nursing home your life was shrunk to a small room, a few bits and pieces you took with you: letters, photographs in envelopes, mass cards. A love note from my father in his barely legible scrawl. *I'm sitting here on Howth Hill*, it said, *and I can't stop thinking about you and wishing you were here with me.*

The television was on and the children were playing that day you collapsed. You'd gone into the other room and we didn't hear you fall. You were lying there on the floor and I thought of a fish landed on a riverbank, fear and incomprehension in your eyes, your mouth open, struggling for breath.

When the ambulance men arrived you joked and flirted with them.

—Your mother is a gas woman, they said.

My sister and I raced behind the ambulance all the way to the hospital, where the doctor told us:

—This time it's not looking good.

There you lay, fingers twitching at the blankets. All the minutes of all your days came to this moment. You always taught us to pray for a happy death at home, surrounded by those who loved you, not among plastic curtains, the smell of hospital and stale piss and humanity, a television blaring a football match, the awful food untouched. The only sign of beauty the window open to the sea in the distance.

Your eyes were closed, the veins in your arms bruised from the needles and drips, your breath ragged. You opened your eyes for a moment and tried to focus on me. I could see your fear.

—Where am I?

—You're at the hospital, you had a bit of a fall.

—My throat is dry.

I took the plastic beaker from beside the bed, raised your head, and you sipped the water and lay back on the pillow, falling again into sleep. I knew by the faces of the nurses and the soft words they said that your condition was grave.

I recalled the last time I'd seen you in the hospital. I had come from New York to be by your side.

—She's a gas ticket, your mother, a great character, said the nurse as I walked into your room.

There you were sitting up in the bed.

—Would you ever get that hair cut, you look like a corner boy, you said.

You felt my jacket.

—Oh, that's good leather, I can always tell the good quality. Would it suit me, do you think?

I helped you out of bed and you tried it on and called in the nurses.

—What do ye think, girls? Does it make me look like Liz Taylor or a bookie at the racecourse? Here, you told me, go and say hello to that woman over there, she's not long for this world.

I shook hands with a feeble old creature wrapped in a shawl, who said:

—Are you a politician? Going around shaking hands and smiling at people?

—It's the tablets, you said, has her not the full shilling, God love her.

A priest had been coming to see you every day.

—A grand little package of a man, from out foreign. Thailand no less. But I think he might be kicking with the other foot if you get my drift, a little on the effeminate side. But sure what about it, isn't he God's anointed and a comfort to me?

You always astonished me, how you could move with the times.

I sat by the bed. You were smaller, the roots of your hair showing through the dye. I thought of the gratitude I owed for what you had given me. Your love of poetry, your love of the sound of words. Yeats, Robert Burns. Your favorite quote was from Shelley. *Fear not the future, weep not for the past.* I try to live by that still.

That last time we sat in a crowded room at a party, you recited Keats:

> *O what can ail thee, knight at arms,*
> *Alone and palely loitering?*
> *The sedge has wither'd from the lake,*
> *And no birds sing.*

Everyone applauded and I realized maybe you had missed your career, that you might have been an actress or a performer of some kind, because you were so alive and so happy in that moment.

Had marriage and children been enough?

I remember a day when you put on your coat, crying:

—I can't take it anymore, I'll go mad. I'm going up the mountains and I'm not coming back.

And we begged: —Don't go, please Mammy.

We never knew why you said that. It was the first time I realized you might have been unhappy.

—Alright, I won't go this time, and you took your coat off, and we held onto you as tight as anything.

Or that day we were walking in the street, and you stopped and pointed at a name over a chemist's shop.

—I could have been married to him, imagine that.

Did that mean I would have had another life as a chemist's boy, or would I have never been born at all? I still think of you standing and looking at that sign, your quietness afterward, making me feel I'd done something to make you unhappy.

Maybe that was the shadow on your soul, the source of your discontent, of that faraway look when you smoked a cigarette or sipped coffee in the Shelbourne. I remembered us cycling home one night from my music lesson, my eight-year-old self in the small carry chair behind you, leaning my sleepy head against your back, holding my snow-covered accordion until we arrived home like snow ghosts, red-nosed and watery-eyed.

Had your faith banished fear of death and what might be beyond? I wanted more than anything for that to be so, for you not to die in fear, which surely you deserved after all the masses and rosaries, for the life of struggle and hardship to pass gently. *Take care of her Padre Pio.*

I hope you were proud of me despite my shortcomings, that I brought you at least some happiness. Forgive my inability to show you love, my impatience, my cruelty in turning away when maybe you needed me the most. I know now your loneliness, your regret that you had been denied the life you should have had, yet I resented your desperate need for me, your silent hurt when I withdrew, and I feared that you would swallow my soul if I allowed myself to open up to you. I closed the door on the real story of my life and denied you intimacy and access. But I still remember you at the most unexpected moments. Even now in this Broadway dressing room, here you are, my mother, in the corner, your ghost never far from the action.

Last night I dreamed that my father was walking in the orchard behind the house in the country, a thin moon overhead. I could see him as if in daylight. He raised his hand in that shy half salute he always gave me, walking in the slightly hunched way that made him seem tentative, like a child entering a room of adults. He always smiled in my dreams, yet this night he seemed perplexed, as though he wondered why he was among the trees in the orchard at that hour. I called out, but he moved away and slowly the air darkened around him.

Then he appeared again, seeming lost, as if looking for something or someone, a coat over his arm, thinner, walking by a wide, still river, all the ghost people there, rows and rows deep, far as the eye could see. He was looking for someone. My mother. And she said, in the dream:

—Don't worry. Look how we smile. We are happy.

Then the river faded, and the trees too, and the sky and the fields, and I watched you both walk back among the apple trees, blossoms raining down.

<hr/>

—Ladies and gentlemen of the company, this is your final call. Please take your places.

Costume on. Fly checked. Breathe. Open the door. Down the stone steps. Other actors are filing out, leaving the safety of their own rooms.

—Be great darling.

—You too.

Silence slowly descends, the house lights dim. In the dark a thousand eyes watch. I wait in the wings. Stepping into a play feels like stepping into a dream, where time is altered by imagination.

The stage is lit now. The music begins. I move toward the light.

Acknowledgments

To Teri Hayden my agent and friend.

Thank you to Elisabeth Schmitz for encouraging me to write this.

Katie Raissian for your guidance and care. (As well as patience for a man who wrote a book on an iPad and lost the first draft).

To the entire Grove team, especially Morgan Entrekin, Deb Seager, Justina Batchelor, Judy Hottensen, Julia Berner-Tobin, Gretchen Mergenthaler, and Sal Destro.

Thanks also to Anna Stein my wonderful literary agent.

The team at Picador UK, especially Ravi Mirchandani, Gaby Quattromini, Gillian Fitzgerald-Kelly, and Katie Green.

To Cormac Kinsella.

Gratitude to my family: Donal, Tom, Breda, and Margaret for their loyalty, love, and sense of humor.

To the memory of my mother Eileen, my father Dan, and Marian my sister, who live on in my heart.

Finally my children Romy, Jack, and Maisie, lights of my life.